THE POWER OF GRIEVING

A Stronger You

MJ Boggini-Atkins, M.Ed., LPC

ISBN: 1450536107
ISBN-13: 9781450536103

For Hank and Jessica Lynlee

In Memoriam

To those who have taught me unforgettable lessons–
especially Nino, Sophie, Charles, Stephen O,
June, Elizabeth, and Olive

Table of Contents

❧

Introduction

❧

It is 1955. A family has lost their precious ten-year-old son. Parents are numb. Siblings are confused. No one is available to explain the aftermath of such a tragedy. Nurses and doctors have whispered the words, "We're sorry." The family drives home from the hospital in silence. From that point on, no one talks about what happened. This silence, along with the confusion and pain, permeates their lives and follows them into the future–echoing the unresolved grief from generation to generation.

This scenario was commonplace for many generations. Individuals who lost their loved ones were left on their own to move through the most difficult passage of their life. More often than not, they were left to bear the pain and consequences of unresolved grief–affecting their lifetimes and the lifetimes of their legacies. That was the grief template taught by our families and culture.

Today we have an abundance of death education information and a profession devoted to helping people move through their grief in a healthy way. A family with a similar situation today can receive guidance and counseling before, during, and after a loss. Yet despite all the helpmates and support systems, we continue to be a society that tends to deny, short circuit or misjudge perfectly normal feelings as abnormal when someone dies. This puts us on the road to unresolved grief, thus complicating our healing process.

The choice to allow the grieving process to unfold lies within all of us. In the midst of tragedy, as we move through excruciating feelings, we realize that, in time, the face of tragedy changes. We have come to understand that this mystery called life can disappear within a blink of an eye. We know our loved ones will always be missed. Our lives are changed forever. Within these undeniable changes we discover our appreciation for the present, the power to heal, the power to rejoin life, and a newfound face that re-defines our strength.

The Power of Grieving is designed to be a guide–your guide–to assist you on your journey from loss to recovery. Information and suggestions are based upon knowledge from experts, my counseling experience and personal journey through loss, as well as from individuals like yourself who share their wisdom and recovery from loss.

Each chapter is short and can be read in order or in any sequence you want. Many messages are repetitive, for when you grieve, your concentration and ability to read may be lessened.

Wherever you are in the grieving process, let your intuition be your guide to what, when, and how much to read. If you follow your own rhythm and timing, you can receive what you most need in your journey toward healing.

This guide is for you–when you are ready–to partner with "The Power of Grieving".

PART I

∾

OVERVIEW OF LOSS

The News and Reactions: Diverse as thumbprints

The Mirror Image: How death and dying touch us

The News and Reactions: Diverse as thumbprints

❧

It is a sunlit day with not a care in the world entering your cloudless sky. In a flicker of a moment, a spoken word of sorrowful news dashes away the brightness of the day, leaving your sky dark, your path uncharted, and no map to follow.

Whatever the news–a sudden death, an accident, a pronouncement of a terminal illness, an abandonment, a divorce, or a disease that only knows its own course–the challenge is to continue your plans, while life demands that you behave differently. You are changed forever.

Each circumstance has its own thumbprint. All will follow a path of mixed emotions. Your experience will not exactly mirror another. It will be yours alone.

Your reaction to any unexpected or unwanted news can be traced to learned patterns from your birth family, cultural expectations, past experiences, and your genetic make-up. Be assured that any reaction that emerges, short of harming yourself and others, is appropriate. There is no right or wrong. Some people are stunned, others are paralyzed, and many are angry. Sometimes you feel physical pain. Old illnesses can resurface. Your back may act up or allergies may return. Depression or anxiety or both can grip you. Some people jabber incessantly or burst out in uncontrollable tears. Still others retreat into their heads, do not feel, and become driven by goal setting and planning their method to move on.

Although some reactions are immediate, it may take moments, days, even months before deep feelings of pain begin to emerge–the ones of sadness, anger, and, at times, hopelessness.

I remember my friend, Carol, who devoted hours to caring for her husband who had been diagnosed with pancreatic cancer. She had a plan of action, took control of any problem and rarely showed any emotion. Months later she was watching a talk show that had to do with illness and she melted into sobs that lasted for hours. Her problem solving and goal setting dissolved as she gave way to delayed feelings.

These reactions you have can flood your senses and disrupt your harmony. This is part of the roller coaster process of grieving. If you can remind yourself that these deep feelings are normal, you will find in time–your time–that grief will lessen and interest in life will return.

The Mirror Image:
How death and dying touch us

ᕐ

When someone dies or is dying, events from your past and raw feelings can resurface in the present. They may appear without warning. Like a mirror in front of you, you are pulled into looking at your own mortality while experiencing your loved one's passing.

The reflection from this mirror can reveal many emotions and behaviors that have influenced your life. Depending on how deeply you look into it, you will see your strengths, fears, anger, ability to forgive, or not to forgive–and hopefully, your ability to love.

I am reminded of the time I was privileged to be among a group of people to be called to the bedside of my friend, June. We surrounded her in what we thought to be her last moments. June displayed all the traits she donned in life–loving, sarcastic, direct, controlling, vulnerable and humorous. Most powerful of all was a scene of forgiveness with a family member. As we watched June let go of years of fear and hostility, we felt we were in the presence of a sacred moment. A lifetime echoed back to the family in a short period of time, erasing the ugly and leaving a slate of forgiveness for all of us to witness, especially her children.

On my drive home from June's house, rain was falling gently, forming small puddles along the road. June had almost slipped away, and yet something profound occurred.

The air was crisp, mingled with the scent of flowers as though a cleansing were ordered by the cosmos. Despite feeling vulnerable and scared with a heightened awareness of *my* mortality, I felt blessed, loved, and grateful.

The scene I had witnessed pushed questions to the forefront of my mind. Will I be as honest when I'm dying? What legacies will I leave behind? What changes could I make now in my life? What is my mission on this earth? What do I need to resolve now and with whom? If you were to answer these questions, what would you say?

I saw my face in the mirror that day. I learned that if we are present to our loved ones in their final journey, even if the relationship is difficult, we can hold this mirror to our face and receive life's greatest lessons. Death, our uninvited teacher, challenges us to live with truth and to love now. Not tomorrow, not the future–but NOW. A powerful reminder that no matter how we live life, the sacred moment is all we have.

PART II

❧

THE CARETAKER

The Caretaker: Giving and receiving

Your Cup Runneth Over: A two–handed journey

Helping Hands: Connect the dots

The Caretaker:
Giving and receiving

∽

You are the caretaker
Caring for yourself
Caring for a loved one
Planning
Making decisions
Not sure when death is coming
Grieving–Knowing that death is near

As a caretaker, you are charting a path with few landmarks. Your life is uprooted. It is in this predicament when you believe death may occur that you simultaneously experience your own grief, the grief of the person who is ill or dying, and the demand to help orchestrate this frightening journey. You are the conductor being challenged to bring it all together.

During this care-giving phase of the journey, you will have a multitude of responses–many of which are unpredictable. These are mixed with days of normalcy and predictability. Generally, feelings of suffering will alternate with hopeful ones. Maybe your loved one will survive. Your hopes are entirely appropriate, as mysteries and miracles that we cannot explain happen all the time. A realistic view of hope should never be discouraged.

During the last months of my friend June's life, she received daily, a special gift from her son. He brewed a particular tea that he heard could cure many diseases if prepared properly. My friend, so touched by her son's caring, accepted this not-so-tasty potion every day, most of the time sharing it with the ivy plant next to her bed. She knew in her heart that she was dying, but by accepting this precious offering from her son, the love between them grew.

This time frame before death is like riding a seesaw–a time when everyone straddles the possibility of hope and the finality of death. As the days move on, it is evident that your job is huge. It is demanding and complex. The balance can change daily. It is not easy to assess your needs and the needs of your loved one. A key to remaining healthy is to understand the balance of giving and receiving. Your cup runneth over and needs to be refilled.

Your Cup Runneth Over:
A two-handed journey

∽

Your everyday living requires energy and stamina to solve and resolve the practical issues of whatever is the work of the day. The added responsibility of care giving demands more from you and requires enormous amounts of energy, planning, and nurturing. You find yourself juggling events and developing skills you didn't know you had.

You may have conflicts with your employment and need to readjust your work schedule. Time for extra-curricular activities may be reduced, and you may have to ask your family for more assistance at home. A crisis point can occur if your care giving is continuous without replenishment. This crisis can manifest itself in physical symptoms, withdrawal, addictive behaviors, depression and anxiety, or acting out with curtness and anger toward others. When you are not in touch with your feelings, you run the risk of hurting the feelings of others. You don't want to be unduly injured, or injure others, especially the person who is dying. You must learn to set boundaries for yourself and to pay attention to your state of health. To avoid a downward spiral, accept the reality that you are not superhuman. You are fallible, vulnerable, and exhaustible. Respect your right to meet your essential needs. Your cup runneth over and needs to be refilled. The important lesson to be learned is to take care of you. Even fifteen minutes a day devoted solely to you can make a huge difference.

My friend, Maggie, cared for her quadriplegic husband for eighteen years. Soon after he died from a blood clot, she was faced with the illness and eventual death of both parents. Her endless devotion and service to those she loved left her exhausted. She received a wake-up call when she was diagnosed with leukemia. With the help of a therapist, Maggie made a conscious decision to face the mental, physical, and spiritual issues of her life. She needed someone to listen to her. Today she is in remission and takes the time to assess her needs and to take care of herself. Her life is moving in an optimistic direction. She feels healthier and allows herself to receive the gifts of love and friendship from the many people whose lives she has touched with her generous spirit.

Sometimes you can find yourself in predicaments when you haven't a clue how to handle a situation. This is the time to ask others who have experienced a similar situation or seek help from professionals and organizations like hospice or homemaker services. One predicament is when the dying person is worried about who will take care of the survivors.

Carrie was the main caretaker for her sister who was dying of cancer. Her sister asked Carrie to help tell her two children that she was dying. She also asked Carrie if she would help her husband raise them. Carrie was dumbstruck. "I can't do this. I'll fall apart. How can I tell them?" She did not feel that she had the capacity or skill to be part of this heart- wrenching process. She called the local hospice and asked for assistance. After discussing how and what to say to the children, Carrie discovered that not only did she rise to the occasion, but she also possessed a strength that she never knew she had.

Not all caretakers or caretaking is charged with continual trauma, pain, and sadness. The in-between moments are packed with "the stuff of life"–theirs and yours.

As you move through the days and weeks, it is easy to be caught up in the blur of responsibility and miss those special moments that, oftentimes, defy words and yet capture your mutual caring. Some are so poignant that the meaning of life and the reason you are here flashes across your mind like a blip on a screen–and then it's gone. You know you understood it, at least for that second, and then another reality emerges, creating the reality of your new "now" and the work of the moment. In those special instants, the sacred moment and the reality of the work become one.

When my friend Arlene was dying, we'd hobble into a movie for our weekly matinee. Oftentimes, it was just the two of us in the theatre, holding each other's arms, the silence deafening, the tears trickling, the sacredness of our friendship permeating every moment. Knowing our time was limited, we sat together in love and pain–not knowing where one left off and the other began.

I remember one afternoon when Arlene called me frantically. She was having trouble breathing and thought this was the end. The doctor told her to go immediately to the emergency room. I rushed out of the house with not a look back in the mirror as to my appearance. I gently put her into the car and headed toward a destination I dreaded. At one point, I looked over and noticed that Arlene was color-coordinated from head to toe and was putting on lipstick to match her outfit, all the while, through her tears, telling me of her fears that her life would not go on much longer. Who would think of vanity at this crucial moment? My friend would. My tension melted. I burst out laughing. We both knew the meaning: as she was concentrating on her appearance, death was not going to be her date at the hospital. When we arrived at the emergency room, the attendant looked at me and asked which one of us needed to be examined.

To this day, I still cherish those moments. They are my comforter of love. As our everyday schedules continue against the backdrop of responsibility, the humor-filled moments wiggle their way into our drama. If we are aware, these gems of grace–rich with the "stuff of life"– are present even in the most difficult circumstances.

Another important lesson to learn is the equation of loving–the ability to receive as well as to give love. If you are doing all the giving and not receiving from the ones you are caring for, what message does this give to them? If you were the patient, how would you feel? Do you not have value until your last breath–and after? Do you not have precious gifts to give your loved ones, no matter what the form? Gifts from loved ones who are infirm or dying reveal themselves in many wrappings–shared feelings with one another, words of wisdom, seeds of advice, a joke, a smile of gratitude, a sigh of knowing, and putting one's affairs in order. If you are present in the relationship, many gifts will appear.

When Arlene was dying, although very weak, she helped me through a difficult time in my life. One time, while caring for her physical needs, she saw a tear run down my face. She stopped me in what I was doing and questioned me with compassion and tenderness. Even though she was unable to move her body, she was fully capable of opening her heart and giving me advice. The equation of loving and giving was a two-handed journey with each of us receiving nurturance.

Two people holding hands is a powerful conduction of energy that flows back and forth from one person to another. One hand extended with giving, the other receiving–both blend into one–indistinguishable. The powerful flow of energy moves through each of you, lending balance and support. As you receive one another's gifts, you remain on equal footing, with no one greater or more important than the other.

Helping Hands:
Connect the dots

～

As you begin to experience your reactions, you realize that the hard road of care giving has become a reality. Here are a few specific and practical things that can ease the struggle.

- Assess your current life situation such as your needs, your family's needs, work responsibilities, and the amount of time you can devote to care giving.
- Accept when people offer to help.
- Ask family and friends what they can contribute; preparing meals, running errands, returning phone calls, sitting with the patient. Make a specific list.
- Choose a few main coordinators who will be the relaters of information. These individuals could devise a schedule for errands to be run, doctors' appointments to be made, times people will sit with the patient, and any other needs to be met. A copy could be e-mailed to each individual. Any changes would be referred back to the main coordinators.

Coordinators can be changed to give a chance for a respite.

- Be sure all doctors and support staff are aware of one another. If not, you connect the dots to make sure they are aware of all the treatments and medications. This ensures the health and safety of the patient. Make a list and distribute it to every caregiver, professional, and support staff involved with the patient.

- Build in time to release your feelings. Any form of exercise, meditation, or massage can be helpful in this process. Do not feel guilty. This is just as important as your care-giving time. You will be rested, relaxed, and more efficient. Fifteen minutes can really make a difference.

- Take time to sit quietly, meditate, or listen to soothing music of your choice. It is in this stillness of time that you marshal your strength and possibly become aware of new ideas and strategies to move you through to the next moment.

- Allow yourself to express tears. They are nature's natural and healthy response to grieving. Releasing them will help you to sleep better and to remove toxins from your system.

- Eat healthier foods consisting of more grains, vegetables, and fruits. Avoid regular bouts of sugar, alcohol, junk food, and nicotine, as these foods can become toxic to your system.

- Ask for hugs. Touch is a reminder that you are cherished and are being supported.

- Feel, or at least verbalize, what you are feeling so you do not put your anger, resentment, and withdrawal behavior onto others. Ask for professional assistance if you feel you are unable to do this on your own.

- Assess your comfort zone. If a task asked of you is painful or makes you feel uncomfortable, be honest and say so. Ask someone else to complete it. Do not see this as a failure. Other people are available who can offer their help. Helping is loving no matter what the form. You need everyone's skills to complete the whole task of care giving.
- Stay in the moment. Your loved one's condition can change daily. Know that change is inevitable. Projecting will only increase your anxiety and take you away from the precious moment.
- Remember that the patient's wishes always take precedence unless health and safety issues are at stake. These are the most controversial areas and are not always clear-cut. If you are unsure of what to do, reach out for professional help.
- Make sure you have someone to listen to you. Your voice, feelings, and frustrations need to be heard.
- Perhaps you can think of more that are unique to your situation.

Remember, by following these suggestions to honor yourself in this difficult process, you are doing the best you can for yourself and others.

PART III

∾

FEELINGS: THE GATEWAY TO RECOVERY

Feelings: What are they? What do we do with them?

Feelings: The phases

Feelings: Finding the balance

Feelings: What you feel is what you heal

Feelings remain: Light returns and
reactions are recognizable

Feelings: What are they?
What do we do with them?

∽

When difficult feelings begin to emerge, what do you do with them? Do you share them? Do you ignore them? Or do you invite them in, allow them to wash over you, and direct your journey toward healing?

How you deal with your emotions is influenced by the present situation, family teachings, the culture, your personality, and the sensitivity of the people around you. You have a choice of when, where, and to whom to express your most intimate sentiments. You could also choose to experience them in solitude as opposed to sharing them. This is a fine line to walk, as too much isolation can add to one's feeling of loss and alienation. The sharing of what you are going through can lighten your burden and open the compassion toward yourself and others.

All that feelings demand of you are to be experienced and to be released without judgment. The key here is not to judge what you feel. These are simply feelings. They do not define your essence or personality. Emotions come and emotions go. They intensify and diminish. Ride them out. Let them teach you. It is when you refuse to experience them that you move into perilous waters. Ironically, the tears that are not experienced are the ones that can drown you. Your strength and courage reside in acknowledging, experiencing, and accepting these momentary truths. Allow the symphony of your grief–energies with different intensities and tones–to play out all its notes. Each piece will come to a completion and around the corner will be the next one–and the next. You will reach a point where these notes of grief will become familiar territory, and, although unwelcomed, your ability to tolerate them and let them flow can surprisingly ease your struggle.

Feelings: The phases

❦

The physical death of your loved one has occurred. A lifetime of memories, including special moments and conversations, are embedded in your mind. Yet the pain of your loss may not be fully recognized or experienced until after weeks, months, or even years have passed. Nature has a way of anesthetizing you with its numbing balm when you need it the most–at a time when you are not ready to feel the anguish. Sometimes, it is too much to take in all at once.

At some point, your bubble of equilibrium bursts. Raw pain washes over you. It can rise up unexpectedly and trigger feelings. You are drenched with the reminder of your loss.

My mother died suddenly of a heart attack the very same day I left on vacation. When I called home, I was given the grave news. Here one moment–and then gone? No words? No good-byes? No final I love you?

After a torrent of tears, I switched into a mode of being in charge. I put away the tissue box. I felt I had no choice. There was work to be done. I was the remaining survivor of my family of four and it was up to me to make decisions and coordinate my mother's funeral. I also had the responsibility of pursuing the legal process of settling an estate, in addition to emptying out a house filled with a lifetime of family memories. Although my emotions surfaced, I had to remain on a course of problem solving.

Two weeks after her death, I was invited to a dinner party where several other couples were in attendance. I thought it would be a good idea to get out and socialize, that the change of pace would help me. How wrong I was. During the dinner, conversation revolved around parents and siblings. My eyes filled with tears, as a knot of sadness was about to explode. I felt my throat tighten and I could barely breathe. These sensations gripped me and provided no outlet. The pain was bone deep. I tried to talk myself out of these sensations, but it was too late. I realized that my feelings did not understand the language of reason. They surfaced when they wanted to. They had drenched me with vulnerability. I composed myself, made an excuse and left early.

I barely made it out the door before tears spilled over me. Although I anticipated a pleasant evening, I received a painful catharsis. I had not been ready to be with company, and I needed some time alone to heal. I had entered the emotional suffering phase of grief.

The intensity and duration of your pain–and when it will come–are dependent upon many factors: the type of relationship you had with your loved ones, the age and the circumstances surrounding their death, your support systems, and whether you have taken the time to grieve or others have allowed you the time to experience your grief. All of these play into your healing. Also, if the relationship has not been a positive one, with many issues unresolved, it may take longer to experience some sense of equilibrium and familiarity of life.

National grief educators Deidre Felton and Sister Teresa McIntier suggest that the time frame is dependent upon your support systems. If individuals are not encouraged to take the time to grieve and are accommodating the needs of others, then their sorrow will be suppressed and the healing will take longer. These are only guidelines because an individual's grieving process is as unique as the individual.

Grieving from deaths such as suicides, murders, terrorist attacks, or other forms of violence will take longer to process. It is advisable to seek help from professionals or from those who have experienced these types of death to guide through these added minefields of human emotion. You can only hope to learn from those courageous souls who have experienced this added trauma and have been able to return to life with some sense of optimism.

Many of these individuals can act as guides, sharing their resiliency and optimism. Victor Frankl's classic book, **Man's Search for Meaning** (Pocket Books, 1976), offers examples of how Holocaust survivors find meaning beyond themselves. John Walsh, the moderator of *America's Most Wanted* television show, whose child was kidnapped and murdered, devotes his time to tracking down the perpetrators of heinous crimes against children.

Endless ways to redefine and add new meaning and experiences to your life are available. My sister-in-law, Jane, is a great example of someone who decided to give her life a new direction and aid others in the process. At the age of forty-six, she became a widow with four grown children. Several years after my brother's death, she decided to materialize a dream she had as a young girl. She went to work for the Peace Corp and Doctors Without Borders, aiding individuals who are victims of war, health, and environmental disasters in Africa and other Third World countries.

When you feel more hopeful about life and your emotions are more in balance, any venue you choose to help others will not only help your grieving process but also aid another in their time of loss. Paying it forward reminds us that we are all interconnected and colors our life with a meaningful perspective.

Regardless of how you choose to add meaning to your life after your loved one has died, the phases you pass through are the same. If you are to return to an appreciation for life, and move on, you need to move through these phases. Grief educators can assist you in understanding the passages you move through after any loss. The following material was written and presented by Sister Teresa McIntier at a bereavement-training program. She summarized the general phases one passes through after any loss.

Intellectual / Shock

Numbness, disbelief, and alienation from others–this is nature's way of protecting the griever against pain too severe to handle all at once. Loss is dealt with on a very rational level. The bereaved is able to talk about the death in an almost clinical manner. Getting stuck in this phase makes one vulnerable to aftershocks later.

Emotional / Suffering

Strong emotions such as anger, fear and guilt come into play. The bereaved may experience bouts of uncontrolled weeping. This is a difficult phase for griever and those around the griever. There is often little or no provocation for emotional outburst.

Reconciliation / Recovery

Begins to rebuild life. If the recovery process is delayed, another problem can set in. Emotional swings slow down. An emotional scar forms and is not as painful to touch. The deceased is never forgotten. Focal point in life now shifts. Life can begin again with renewed energy and understanding.

These three phases are like developmental stages you must pass through. If you miss, deny, or ignore any of them, especially the emotional/suffering phase, a future loss will beckon you back with another invitation for these grief feelings to emerge.

Feelings: Finding the balance

༄

In my profession, having talked with people over a thirty five-year period and having heard hundreds of heartfelt stories, I know why it can be a struggle to deal with difficult feelings. It takes time, it can hurt, and it can bring you to recognize some truths that are painful. Accompanying these thoughts are the fears that you will remain stuck and not move on, be considered weak, become a burden, lose friends, and, perhaps, never be happy again.

A gentleman I met at a conference talked about how his father cried over the smallest thing. He could never solve problems and would get lost in his emotions. He didn't respect this aspect of his father, so he chose the opposite behavior. In addition, he grew up in the John Wayne era and believed the philosophy that heroes and winners act tough, don't show feelings, and never cry. "It took me almost forty years to understand how I choked off important feelings and aspects of my life because I was afraid I'd become like my father. As a consequence, I shut off meaningful communication with my family. And then, of course, there's that "macho thing."

Pat, a client of mine, reflected the opposite scenario of denying feelings. She continued to experience every nuance and emotion endlessly. These emotions mirrored her negative, hopeless thoughts. Eventually, the unrelenting angst projected onto her friends began to affect her relationships. A friend took the initiative to encourage Pat to seek professional help. Today, by practicing positive thinking, coupled with realistic problem solving, she is learning to let go of needing to feel and express everything to everyone. Her task is to let go of perpetual emotions. It is as difficult for her to diminish her drama as it is for the gentleman to learn to express his feelings.

One person in grieving avoids feelings; the other gets so caught up in it, she cannot move on with her life. You can feel either too much or too little. The challenge in dealing with difficult feelings is to find a balance between the two. Continually revolving around in feelings or closing the door on them are both patterns that can keep you stuck. In order to move on with your life, it is necessary to balance and partner your emotions and problem-solving skills with physical activity. Solve the problems you can and let go of the rest. Easier said than done, but by practice and perseverance you will feel less pain, feel more in control, and in some fortunate moments, there will be an ease within the struggle.

Feelings: What you feel is what you heal

The process of healing resides in the domain of feeling. The road of grief is not a straight line or a neatly paved highway. It is a raw course that opens you up to all the truths and consequences of your experiences with your loved one. No shortcuts or detours exist. It is predictably unpredictable. At any moment an overflow of recognizable or unrecognizable feelings can surprise you. You may alternate among tears, anger, bewilderment, depression, lethargy, and anxiety. You may have flashbacks, nightmares, or feelings of dissociation; feel as though you are going crazy without a secure place to find comfort. This can be very scary. Physically, your body reacts. Muscles and bones may ache, limbs may feel cold, and your heart may feel numb or hurt. When your heart hurts, you fear that it will never stop aching or that someone has stolen it from you forever.

Addictions previously under control may resurface. Overeating, undereating, alcohol consumption, drug abuse, endless shopping, or flitting from one thing to another are all ways of running away from yourself–not allowing yourself truthful feelings. I know a woman who, after her husband's death, ran from mall to mall buying needless clothes and charging up a storm. She became a dizzying storm of movement in order to avoid her feelings. What she ended up with was an expensive wardrobe in addition to the lingering pain.

Trauma and loss can even reflect sympathetic symptoms. This is when you believe that you are mimicking the same symptoms or illness from which your loved one died. David was twenty-one when his father died of a brain tumor. He began to have excruciating headaches and became convinced he had the same illness. He went to the doctor and after a series of tests, discovered that fear and exhaustion were the underlying cause. As soon as the doctor assured him that nothing was wrong, his symptoms abated. David was wise to see a doctor. Physical symptoms can signal that something is wrong.

Understand that your mind can be vulnerable to suggestion during this difficult period. You could be watching a play at the theater and the actor's words strike sadness. The words become the voice of your loved one. A familiar song or the smell of a loved one's favorite food can reduce you to tears. It is possible that you may even hear the voice or see visions of the deceased. This can provide comfort or elicit fear or you can vacillate between these two emotions. One time when I was in a supermarket, I spotted a man who looked like my deceased brother. I followed him around for over fifteen minutes. My heart wanted it to be him yet my head knew the truth. My longing to reunite with my brother led me to follow a strange man up and down supermarket aisles.

If at any time in this process you feel frightened by your behavior or question whether your experiences are within the normal range, by all means, talk to someone who has been through grieving or speak with a professional, or do both. In some situations, medication may be recommended as a helpmate to move through this period.

You must remember that your emotions, like the path of a river, should not be forced or halted. You can only follow them where they take you, feel them, talk about them, and especially honor them. Just as a river finds new channels of discovery–so, too, will your feelings.

Feelings remain: Light returns and reactions are recognizable

❧

At some point in the stages of grief, the thick fog of mourning starts to lessen. The days do not seem to be as dark and light begins to emerge. A familiar feeling of comfort emerges, and you begin to recognize the seasons of life.

You are now becoming familiar with the terrain of grief. Emotions of the moment are not so upsetting. You find that you don't burst into tears when you hear the person's name. A wife is able to speak with humor about her deceased husband without sobbing. A son can finally muster the courage to be a speaker at his father's yearly testimonial. He finds himself capable of feeling his own strength and understanding his father's legacy. Recycling these familiar feelings with less intensity becomes the norm. Your barometer feels more balanced and your stamina increases steadily.

Three years ago, Myra, a colleague, lost her husband to a sudden death. The first year of mourning was filled with tears and, at times, feelings of dissociation. She felt detached from herself and the world. She survived the first round of holidays but with great dread as each one triggered her intense loneliness. After several years of painful holiday celebrations, however, she devised ways to ease this pain. She drove her car, in case she wanted to leave the group early, arrived later in the day, helped with serving food and cleaning up, played with the children, and sat next to a person whom she trusted and could talk to. Today Myra can still feel those unexpected pangs but knows that they will not last. She has become a veteran of having several holidays under her belt. And every year she becomes more comfortable in recognizing trigger situations and knowing how to handle them. During the holidays she is surprised that the grief moments aren't as intense and actually finds that she is beginning to enjoy these occasions more. She is better equipped to respond to the unexpected triggers or the novel ones when they occur. This transition indicates that she is moving through the mourning phase.

In his book, **Grief Counseling and Grief Therapy** (Springer Publishing Co., Inc., 2001) William J. Worden explains the four tasks of mourning.

- To accept the daily loss
- To work through the pain of loss
- To adjust to environments in which the person/object is missing
- To relocate and memorialize the loved one

When your life begins to operate in a more predictable pattern, you are getting your energy back for life. You wonder if the feelings of intensity are gone for good. The answer is yes and no. The intensity and duration of painful feelings will subside in time if you allow yourself to move through the stages of mourning. The more painful feelings can resurface and recycle, especially during anniversary dates, holidays, and sometimes for no discernible reason–they just will. Yet your ability and understanding to ride them out is more hopeful as you know that they are temporary visitors.

I can remember preparing dinner for friends one month after my father died and hearing the song, "The Wind Beneath My Wings," on the radio. The lyrics triggered all my loss feelings. To this day, when I hear this song, I may still cry as my wounds surface. So be it: I have learned to accept this experience and recover, without feeling that I am stuck in grief. These musical notes may make me weep, but they also give me comfort.

So these wounds will never go away completely, but they should not control your life. They are part of remembrance, the light in your life giving you a nudge to see what is directly in front of you. Embrace the moment. Connect with the living. These moments can light the way to the deepest part of yourself and connect you to a place where you have that special knowledge, a wordless understanding of connection to all.

This sacred place of healing can draw you closer to everyone who has experienced or will experience a loved one's passing. This legacy of light lives within you and can reach out to others and serve as an example to return to life–scars and all. When you choose to face your difficulties, confront your emotions, move through the best and the worst of times–you give meaning to your life. You honor yourself. You become the one in control–and stronger.

PART IV

◈

TAKING CHARGE

Making Peace with the Unresolved: Stuck in the muck

Guidance is Available: Choices

Move with, Feel, Let go, and Continue on, Move with...

Stepping Back into the World

Religion, Spirituality, and Ritual: Remembrance
and connection

Making Peace with the Unresolved: Stuck in the muck

∽

Whenever you suffer a loss, you are vulnerable. You can feel helpless and acknowledge that you have no control over how, when, or where your loved ones are taken from you. You are left with much unresolved.

An acceptance of death becomes more integrated into your understanding of life if the relationships have been positive, or if the not-so-positive fences have been mended before the loved one dies. Difficulty unfolds when you feel that something in the relationship was never finished. You may carry these burdens in your heart. The guilt on your shoulders may be heavy.

What if you never liked the person? What if you had an unresolved fight with your loved one before he died? What if you were never appreciated for who you are? What if your behavior was not loving? What if you were never given thanks for your care giving? What if you never had the opportunity to say goodbye to the dying person? What if you were emotionally, physically, or sexually abused?

What if your loved one was murdered, kidnapped, or met with some horrible sudden death, accident, or suicide? What if...?

Any of these possibilities has the power to slow down your healing and prevent you from moving through the necessary phases of grief. Lack of emotional expression, denial, addictive behavior, constant busyness, or avoidance to talk about the deceased can be red flags of warning that your grieving is halted.

If you continue to resent or cloak yourself in denial, a veneer will form over your heart that will make it difficult to break through to your loving feelings–for your loved ones and for yourself. If you do not work toward a resolve when the next death occurs–and it will–what will flow forth, perhaps in even a greater degree, can be deeper feelings of helplessness and pain. Other manifestations can show up in the realm of physical or emotional symptoms, communication problems, withdrawal in relationships, or lethargy toward life. The holding on to that which is unresolved will become the driving force of your personality rather than a part that surfaces normally and intermittently.

To be able to let go and to not obsess over an unresolved situation, take a look at the family into which you were born. It is helpful and important that you come to terms with your family patterns over the years and past generational history. Even your patterns of current behaviors warrant keen observations. What are the messages and teachings your parents and grandparents passed on? Are they healthy or unhealthy? Do they serve you in a positive way today? Are there traditions, quirks, or fears that we handed down from one generation to the next? This observation will help you to understand and become aware of how you may be continuing certain destructive patterns– and to your magnificent credit, which ones you've stopped.

You learn a multitude of skills from your birth family–communication, problem solving, and general orientation toward life. Many dysfunctions such as alcoholism, denial, the holding onto grudges, workaholism, or abuse of any form can undermine your sense of self-worth, career goals, or relationships. They can affect or shut down your grieving response.

The object is not to blame your family. We all come from a mixture of function and dysfunction. Rather, you need to be aware, to understand the foibles, and to let go of harmful patterns that continue to affect your life. When you do that, you are better able to identify any form of love and constructive behavior that you might have learned from your family. This information can help you and your family to lead healthier lives and to communicate better.

Some family backgrounds are more difficult to translate into the positive. To decide not to pass on negative behavior is a powerful choice. Some of our greatest politicians, artists, humanitarians, and, perhaps, more relevantly, you, come from the most challenging backgrounds. You may be someone who has been tested endlessly by life and, yet, continues to reflect love and hope to those you encounter. Celebrate your strength of character.

A dysfunctional family that consisted of five children was challenged with a lot of issues. The behavior of Al, the father, placed extraordinary stress on the family. Problems ranged from financial instability to workaholism, alcoholism, extramarital affairs, and physical and emotional abuse to family members. The mother did not confront any of her husband's behaviors–a classic case of denial. Neither did the children. When, how, and whom to love remained confusing. Life was chaotic and difficult.

The family continued with their own patterns of survival and denial until one day, when Al, in a drunken stupor, injured one of the children so severely he was hospitalized. Stunned and humiliated, the father left the family. Periodically, he sent hate letters blaming them for his behavior. His threatening letters intensified until one day, they stopped. One week later, the family was notified that he had been killed in a car crash. The other driver was drunk.

How could his family possibly find a way to make peace with this situation? How could anyone? Not only did they have to grieve the loss of a man who wreaked havoc in their lives, but they also felt stunned by the injustice and the irony surrounding his death.

The lid of sanity began to loosen as family members began to show a variety of signs of disruption. Drinking, drugs, and abusive behavior surfaced. A school counselor directed the unraveling family toward the appropriate resource, a professional counselor whose specialization included family dynamics, addiction, and abusive relationships. It took sharing among all of them and a willingness to explore and understand their backgrounds and patterns of behavior to understand what positive choices they could make in their lives so as not to repeat the problems of the past. A lifetime of tears poured forth from everyone.

In addition to counseling, the family sought other disciplines to aid in recovery. Some of the family members increased their exercise. Others signed up for art and music classes, stress management, yoga and meditation classes.

The family is still a work in progress, and always will be. They are making headway and are now able to remember and to love some of the healthy aspects of Al. They recognize that the denial of many generations can be stopped when they chose to become aware of the problems and then move toward a solution. In their situation, the death of Al lifted a coma of frozen feelings and, unexpectedly, ripped them open. Ultimately, their loss gave them the gift of awareness to change.

The insensitive treatment by those who have hurt you, especially when they are dying, is another example of an unresolved relationship. You, once again, have the choice whether to dig deeper to understand their behavior. It is you, and only you, who can understand what has been the problem and what part you play in the scenario. This gives you the power to speak the truth, at least to yourself, to make amends and to establish boundaries so that the person is not abusive in word or deed. This does not mean you need to forget what your insults and injuries are. It does mean that these feelings will harm your body, mind, and spirit if you continue to focus on keeping them alive. Those with whom you've had difficulty will continue to rent space in your head. Your heart will be heavy if you keep the negative patter of their voices alive.

You need never invite abusive relationships into your life, because you will pay the price. To avoid this takes courage, feeling, thoughtful analysis, and being alert to what is occurring in the moment.

Always remember that loving, respecting, and forgiving yourself is the basis for loving, respecting, and forgiving others.

When my friend John's father was dying, he refused to speak to his son. At most, his father would grunt a few words of thanks when he was given something to eat. Their family history was filled with physical and emotional abuse. On many occasions, John tried to talk to his father about the past and their uncomfortable relationship. When he realized his father was not going to engage in any conversation, he decided to write a letter to him and tell him how he felt about their lives together. He waited until his father was in a relaxed, sleepy state to read aloud this summary of his thoughts. John said that he never felt loved, that he felt he was robbed of his childhood and put in a position to be the caretaker of his mother and his brother. He also told his father that, although, he forgave him, he would never forget his abusive behavior. He was, however, able to thank his father for the few good times he could remember. At that point, his father held up his hand to indicate for him to stop reading, but John continued on. When John saw tears stream down his father's face, he knew the message was received.

It is not always advisable to confront those who have hurt you. You are taking a risk to possibly receive another rejection of love. It is a decision that has to be weighed out. Only you can make it. An alternative is to write a letter to that person and not send it. A healing can still occur. If you are in doubt how to handle a situation, ask for guidance, but, ultimately, the choice is yours.

In John's case, a catharsis did occur. His father's tears were a turning point in John's life. Several months later, he shared his thoughts with his mother. He talked about how determined he was–because of the pain he experienced in childhood–to become a better parent and father. "I know that from time to time I will experience some ugly feelings, but they will not bury me. I was controlled long enough by that man."

Whatever situation you need to resolve, you have every right to your stronghold of feelings. However long you decide to entertain them is up to you. The consequences remain clear. You have a choice of movement vs. stagnation, cynicism vs. optimism, love vs. fear, and, ultimately, cherishing the remainder of your life vs. regretting it.

If you need help to resolve old wounds, trained counselors are available to assist you. Support groups and survivors who mirror what you experienced can lend empathy. You are the only one who can take the first step of the journey–a journey that will help you to heal and recognize the gifts from the rubble of your past.

Guidance is Available: Choices

༄

The aftermath of a death can leave you confused and wondering what to do with sad and sometimes excessive thoughts. You can feel like a ship without a rudder floating endlessly without direction. Many venues can help you to understand your thoughts, give you comfort and a sense of structure while moving you through the grieving process. Write in a journal, play a musical instrument, draw, paint, take up drumming, explore a new hobby, or set your body in motion through a sport, Pilates, yoga, or dance.

After my mother died, as I stood by her gravesite, a poem formed in my mind. At the time, this spontaneous poetry gave me a sliver of perspective, helping me to recognize the reality of the moment and to release my feelings.

> *My tear fell on her casket this morning.*
> *It dropped strong and clear.*
> *Its reflection shown the day of mourning to be*
> *simply another day.*
> *Birds flew, cats meowed people ate*
> *And I cried.*

If you don't find these modes of expression helpful or able to give you comfort, by all means, seek out family, friends, or professional help to guide you through your grief. Sometimes talking to a counselor trained in loss can assure you that what you are experiencing is typical. The guidance you choose, if and when you choose it, should reflect your needs, issues, type of loss, physical state of health, and present life situation.

If, however, you find yourself repetitively talking the same painful talk without reprieve, or if your mind is swirling with obsessive thoughts or images, it is imperative to ask for professional assistance. You should also have a physical in order to rule out any systemic problem. In addition to seeking traditional medicine, there are other paths to pursue such as integrative medicine, naturopathic medicine, homeopathic medicine, or acupuncture to help you move toward balance and wellness.

Promising research, to date, indicates that some therapies are more effective change agents if you have experienced and continue to have painful flashbacks, ongoing depression, extreme anxiety, or any complex grieving situation. Some of these are cognitive behavioral therapy, dialectical behavior therapy, neuro linguistic programming, eye movement desensitization reprocessing, hypnotherapy, energy medicine, emotional freedom technique, thought field therapy, and, sometimes medication. Every person is unique, and no one therapy will work for all. More information can be found in the resource section.

Remember, grieving is not a problem to be solved. It is a universal journey that eventually is taken by all of us, and sometimes we need that helping hand.

Move with, Feel, Let go, and Continue on, Move with...

∾

When you face a loss, the truth of *your* life hits you hard. You are aware that if you move on to the invitation of life, your loved one is dead: if you don't move on and reunite with life, your loved one is dead. The reality does not change; you live your life while your loved one cannot.

It is a common experience that if you stop feeling awful, you may believe that the depth of your love was not strong and the connection to your loved one is waning. Nothing could be further from the truth. Because of this mindset, you may feel guilty and be pulled back into pools of grief rather than follow the natural course of mourning— a course that moves you toward the possibilities of joy and opportunity surrounding you. You need to feel without self-judgment.

When you straddle this moving-through/not-moving-through stage, you can feel like a tightrope artist walking from one end of the wire to the other. You may sense that you are in balance, yet within that sensation is that ever-grabbing black hole of grief. You start. You stop. You go back and forth–sometimes feeling the balance and other times grieving in one spot. You wonder whether you will make it. Eventually, you reach the other end of the wire after many starts and stops. Although these black holes of pain will emerge from time to time, you need to move with the grief, feel it, let it go, then continue on, regardless of the ambiguous feelings you may have. Notice the wisdom of nature to see the continual renewal process always in motion. Leaves change and seasons reappear. It is the cycle of life doing what it does best–encouraging movement, promoting change and having faith that renewal occurs.

Your loved ones would not want you to dwell on their illness or belabor the painful unhealthy moments of their life. What if they caused you pain during your life? The best you can do is honor their good points and not repeat their harmful patterns into your life. If you continue to dwell on the negative, the person most hurt will be you.

Consider if the roles were reversed. Would you want your family and friends to be able to appreciate your entire personality by balancing your shortcomings and frailties with your good deeds and strengths? Remember, the difficult details of anyone's life must be understood in perspective within the context of their family history, genetics, and lifetime experiences. Find a way to identify the positives and move forward.

After her mother's death, Wendy was very depressed and could only think about the negative aspects of their relationship. Several months of cognitive behavioral therapy helped her to realize that the negative and unrealistic thoughts about her mother and herself were related to her anxiety and depression. She finally understood that her depression kept her connected to the relationship, and if

Wendy didn't feel sad, she interpreted that to mean her love for her mother was not strong.

Only when Wendy sought professional counseling was she able to begin to understand the roots of her mother's behavior and why this influenced her to make some unhealthy choices in her life. Wendy's angry feelings began to give way to all the other feelings attached to grief–especially sadness. And to her surprise, love!

Eventually, Wendy was able to put her mother's life in a context that was more realistic. She began to understand the many positive things she had received from the relationship and became aware that if she changed the negative thoughts in her head, her emotions would simultaneously become more positive. Today, she moves through life with an awareness of how her thoughts and feelings create her behavior. Wendy appreciates life and even welcomes the moments of sadness that may suddenly surface.

Life reflects a balancing act of mixed experiences that can lead to many lessons. When you are aware of these honest and mixed encounters with your loved one, you can decide to let go of the ones that do not serve you and savor the ones that add strength and wisdom to your life.

Life invites you to move with, feel, let go, and continue on....move with, feel, let go, and continue on…move with, feel, let go, and continue on…..

Stepping Back into the World

An important part of the grieving process is transitioning back into the world, returning to everyday tasks, socializing, or whatever you were doing before this sudden moment took you away from the world as you knew it.

You feel your soul is being tugged at. You may still feel stuck in the past, straddling the ghosts of memories, worrying how you will live out your future without your loved one, you are being pulled at by society to join the moment of now.

Your friends call and want you to feel better.
You want to feel better.
Your family wants you to act "normal."
You want to act "normal."
You are invited to step back into the
world and socialize.
You want to step back into the world.
Or do you? Finding the balance of grieving and
returning to life is not easy.

One week after Judy's husband died, her niece was due to be married. Judy struggled whether to attend, fearful of not being able to keep from crying, yet she loved her niece and had been looking forward to celebrating the day. Although she was nervous, she decided to attend. She needed to excuse herself several times to regain her composure. yet to her surprise, Judy discovered she was capable of experiencing both joy for her niece and sadness for herself at the same time. She called upon her inner strength to allow both feelings to the surface and was successful.

So life continues to play out as we are grieving. Our positions can switch in an instant, and they do. When you grieve the loss of your loved one, someone else celebrates the gift of life.

A grandfather is dying as his granddaughter
is being born.
A couple unites while their friends divorce.
A man receives a promotion while his brother
is diagnosed with a terminal illness.
The sun continues to shine as the winds blow cold.

Religion, Spirituality, and Ritual: Remembrance and connection

∽

Your inner resources and your philosophy of life help you to cope with death. How you interpret death reflects your background of experiences, religious, or spiritual beliefs. These beliefs provide a foundation of support that allows you to exercise your free will and determination to move through the phases of grieving.

If your belief system is rooted in the philosophy that nothing exists beyond this earth, you can use your free will to determine how you play out the rest of your life. Whichever candle you choose to light–religious, spiritual, or a community of friends and family to support you– remember that you are the ultimate designer of your heart and mind; it is within your power to choose your angels of support.

However you choose to remember your loved one, it is the ritual that helps to bridge the gap from loss to remembering. Rituals are the threads of connection to your loved ones. They are a form of mourning that offers the continual comfort, to weave together your memories and to seal your bonds forever. They can be formal or informal; spontaneous or planned; performed alone or with like-minded individuals. They can take place in a church, synagogue, mosque, teepee, golf course, home, nature, or in your heart. You can plant a garden, compose a poem or a piece of music, draw a picture, or simply light a candle. It is not as important what you do as the act of doing it.

Another ritual can involve a ceremony or event that is authentic and reflects the deceased person's life. My brother was an avid golfer, and now his family honors his memory yearly by hosting a golf tournament with the proceeds going to a charity for young people. Another family honors the memory of their sister and gathers together on her birthday each year, cooking her favorite meal and sharing stories of her life. A client honors her deceased husband by lighting a candle every evening before dinner and acknowledging three things she is grateful for in her life.

One of my greatest comforts was being able to create a personal ceremony to honor and reflect my mother's life. I wrote the eulogy and some family members shared memories. One of my mother's favorite songs was played on the piano and sung by a friend of hers. At the end of the ceremony, I passed out a gladiola to each person–a flower that represented her joy and love of the land. Being part of and planning the ceremony brought me great comfort and a feeling of belonging and completion.

It is even possible that the dying person may want to organize the ritual or funeral. My friend June planned her funeral in the same way she orchestrated every day of her life. Before she died, she gave away her precious pieces of jewelry and clothing to her loved ones. Then she picked out her favorite outfit for her funeral and decided whom she wanted to sing, to play the guitar, and to speak about her life. In her last days, she gathered by her side the people she wanted near to her.

At June's funeral, we all played the parts she had hoped we would. On that day, I felt she was guiding me and wrapping her arms around me. I could never have imagined being able to address over four hundred people and not be nervous or grief stricken. As I spoke, I felt as though I were lifted into a state of grace with a sense of connection and peace to all those who sat before me. Any ritual or ceremony that is authentic can remind you that the past and the present connect in your heart forever.

PART V

∽

WHAT EXPERTS SAY

The Body and Mind: Connections and
consequences in grieving

The Mind: How to be in charge

Healing Tears: Nature's medicine drops

Journaling: Therapy on paper

Breathing and the Relaxation Response: Grieving's balm

The Body and Mind: Connections and consequences in grieving

❦

To understand how grieving affects you, it is important to understand the body/mind connection–a complicated and much-debated subject. Let's take some time to briefly understand what the latest research can teach you about moving in a positive direction toward recovery.

Many groundbreaking discoveries and a great deal of research on the body/mind connection and how it affects our health have been conducted over the years and will continue. This is called the field of psychoneuroimmunology. If you are interested in probing into the scientific information, many authors and scientists such as Justin Blair, Drs. Joan and Miroslav Boryshenko, Deepak Chopra, Antonio Domasio, Dr. Wayne Dwyer, Ken Dychtwald, Donna Eden, Dr. David Feinstein, Dr. Richard Gerber, Dr. James Oschman, Dr. Candace Pert, Francis Schmitt, Dr. Bernie Siegel, and Dr. Esther Sternberg, to name a few, can educate you on this topic.

Neuroscientist Candace Pert, Ph.D., who was chief of brain biochemistry at the National Institutes of Health in the '70s, is currently a neuropharmacologist at the Georgetown University School of Medicine in Washington, D.C. Her discovery of the opiate receptor in 1972 revolutionized the Western perspective on where emotions reside in the body. Before this discovery, scientists viewed the brain as the center of the emotions. In her book, **Molecules of Emotion: The Science Behind the Mind/Body Medicine** (Simon and Schuster, 1999), Dr. Pert states that the receptor sites for emotions can be found in all cells of the body, not just the brain. Her book lends clarity to this new paradigm of body/mind communication, that the brain and body cannot be separated. They operate as one in conjunction with the other. The body expresses what the mind thinks or feels–and the reverse is true.

Try this exercise: Think about running your finger down a blackboard. Then imagine eating your favorite ice cream. Now picture hearing the siren of an ambulance. What just happened to you? What was the reaction to the blackboard? Could you feel the taste of ice cream? Did you feel the sirens jolt your body? Did whatever you thought or felt during the process affect your entire system?

So anytime you experience negative thoughts, the brain chemicals will move through your body and bind to receptor sites in your specific organs. Listen to the statements, "I have a gut feeling"; "It hits me right in the gut"; "This makes me hot under the collar"; "That makes my skin crawl"; "My heart aches"; "What a pain in the neck he is." These thoughts, although coming from your head, can translate into physical symptoms.

The repression of negative emotions such as anger and resentment can also lead to physical symptoms. These suppressed thoughts can become toxic and flood your body, especially your stomach, with stress hormones that can manifest or exacerbate existing physical problems. You could experience nausea, anxiety, intestinal upset, or other symptoms. The stomach is often referred to as "the second brain."

This does not mean you dump your anger and run. Anger must be expressed constructively and appropriately for you to resolve problems. When you do express your emotions respectfully, you retain your integrity and your system remains healthier.

For many years my neighbor, Karen, experienced debilitating migraine headaches. After examining what was happening in her life, she identified areas that had bothered her for years. In short, what she resisted persisted. She ended up with a head full of toxic thoughts. She had been harboring intense anger and resentment toward her parents, who had been dead for years. She transferred this hostility to everyone around her. She blamed everyone in her life for her "bad luck," especially her parents. She could not let go. She either suffered from migraines or went on screaming rampages. If she screamed, her head didn't hurt. If she had a migraine, she didn't have the strength to rage. Her doctor recommended that she see a biofeedback counselor–also trained in grief work.

After three months, Karen discovered that beneath all the venom were enormous hurts, misunderstanding, and sadness. When she began to release a flood of tears, her healing journey began. What she discovered was that she never grieved her parents deaths and because of this, became stuck in a toxic pattern of blaming everyone else in her life for what went wrong. For Karen, her headaches were a result of many repressed emotions. Her grieving process was delayed and it wasn't until many years later that she experienced the effects of what had always been there waiting to express itself. As her real emotions began to surface, her headaches began to lessen.

The body/mind interaction continually affects your grieving process. Lyn Prashant M.A, F.T., Ph.D. conducts what she calls terms Degriefing Process™ for people in grief. On her website she explains that the body and mind are linked, therefore techniques must be used to include both physical and mental treatments. In addition to these treatments, self-care techniques can be taught to promote the healing process, which can help when future loss appears.

Stephen E. Owens, doctor of integrative medicine and past chairman of the Capitol University of Integrated Medicine in Washington, D.C., echoes these sentiments. Owens states, "The developing field of integrative medicine reflects the connectivity of all life. All of our systems–immune, nervous, endocrine, cardiovascular–are all communicating and interacting with one another and are continually affecting our emotions. Our reaction to stress affects our level of health. Grieving like any other emotion is appropriate and cleansing provided it resolves itself. It can be resolved with the aid of body, mind, and nutritional therapies. If relief is not experienced, the unresolved stress can worsen our disease."

From this group of experts and others in the field of body/mind medicine, we understand a most important concept. The blending of beliefs, thoughts, emotions, environment, and genetics is similar to a quilt–interwoven and patched together, creating the blueprint for our health–and our future.

The Mind: How to be in charge

❧

"Energy follows thought. We move towards but not beyond what we can imagine. What we assume, expect, or believe creates, colors our experience. By expanding our deepest beliefs about what is possible, we can change our experiences of life."
Dan Millman, **Way of The Peaceful Warrior**

If energy follows thoughts and thoughts are created in your mind, then it is crucial to be aware of what you are thinking. The thoughts that you form–your inner dialogue–create your behavior, and consequently, determine the quality of your life.

Sometimes, your thoughts and feelings partner well in this dance of body/mind communication. You are led into positive thought-affirming territory. Other times, you are caught blindly spinning into a territory that resonates to a negative beat, one that can lead you into places that follow outdated thoughts, messages, and judgments from your past.

At age sixty-five, Rick is an incredible racquetball player. He visualizes and thinks positive statements before he faces his opponents. He sees himself methodically and specifically placing shots to certain areas in the court. Most often, Rick is victorious. However, as a young person he did not have the athletic confidence that he has today. He remembered a time when his coach told him he would never be a great athlete. Because of this comment, Rick hesitated to play sports for most of his life. One day, a friend told him about a creative visualization workshop and he signed up. He credits this course with changing his thinking process and his life. "Success has a lot to do with what you think. I had too many negative messages from authority figures in my head when I was young."

These mother, father, brother, sister, teacher, preacher messages can repetitively clamor in your mind without your awareness. Although many of these are positive and encourage self-esteem, the sometimes negative ramblings often reflect the fragile self-esteem, projections, and judgments of authority figures from your past who have passed on these messages to you. It has more to do with the way that they saw the world; yet you take them in as the truth about yourself. They become easily embedded in your mind and cause you to have poor self-definition. "You'll never amount to anything"; "You're lazy"; "You'll never make any money"; "Women should always defer to men"; "You're just like your no good father"; "Don't be a cry baby"; and "Nothing will ever get better" are all examples of self-destructive thoughts. Generations of our families may have perpetuated this cycle of negative thoughts that you've accepted as truths. The intentions of your families, albeit generally filled with love and good will, can unintentionally pass on negative or fearful messages from a level that escapes your awareness and theirs. It takes an intentional awareness and some action to break this cycle.

During the phases of grieving, your feelings, images, and thoughts will break through with great intensity, oftentimes threatening to overwhelm you. A year after her father died, Elizabeth recalls preparing a meal for a dinner party when she was suddenly overcome with feelings of dread and insecurity. Long before her father's death, she completed a course where she learned to question repetitive thoughts that evoked strong feelings. As she stood at the stove stirring shrimp scampi, she understood that the act of cooking transported her back to a time when she was a teenager and decided to cook a meal for the family. Elizabeth, in her mind, vividly heard her father's comment, "You cook food that a dog wouldn't eat." Within minutes, she put down the pan of scampi, challenged the comment by doing some deep breathing, and replaced the negative reaction with a positive one. She changed it to, "I am a creative cook and a dog should be so lucky to lick my plate." Then she put on some music and started dancing. Although she felt sad over her father's death, she challenged this intrusive, ugly thought and did not allow it to intensify and ruin her dinner party.

When old messages from your authority figures come up in your head, you need to question them to see if they are adding to your grief rather than supporting your process to grieve. Although it may feel strange and difficult to question these familiar and repetitive thoughts, doing so can help you to break a cycle of messages that are not helpful.

Repetitive and negative thoughts can come to mind anytime in your life, not just in the grieving process. A good way to become more aware of yourself is to become a regular listener to your thoughts.

Try this exercise: Be aware of what you are saying to yourself. Do a periodic check, perhaps once every hour or more often. Stop what you are doing and tune into your thoughts. What are you thinking at that moment? If you are having a conversation and someone is not listening to you, do you tell yourself you're boring, a bad conversationalist, and shy? Could it be that the other person is the rude one with poor conversational skills? Challenge yourself to stop and tune into what you just thought and to become a regular listener to yourself. Awareness and creativity are the key. Keep practicing this. The more you try this technique, you will discover a familiar beat and pattern. Is your tendency one of negativity, blame, or outdated belief systems that don't fit the current you? Or does it reflect a pattern of your need for power, security, or approval? Recognize what the messages are and give yourself a choice: to play them if they're positive, not play them if they're negative, change them to new messages, or simply to let them be without judgment.

After Robert filed for bankruptcy, he was having a difficult time. He was depressed, and his anxiety was growing stronger, affecting his self-esteem and his ability to be positive about job hunting. When he learned to tune into the thoughts in his mind, he was surprised at how negative they really were. "I've lost everything"; "I'm a loser"; "I'll never get another job." These ramblings occupied valuable space in his mind and directed his behavior. To counter this negativity, he used several techniques. "There it goes again," or "Isn't that interesting?" were phrases he repeated to himself without judgment whenever the thoughts crept into his head.

Another technique was to use visualization whenever he had these negative thoughts. His girlfriend suggested that if he had such thoughts, he should picture them as ducks swimming by. Or sometimes he chose to see a big red stop sign in his head, tug on his ear, or tap his fingers when he wished to stop the thought.

Robert, like Elizabeth, could also choose to change the negative thought to a positive one. This is called an affirmation. An affirmation is stated in the positive, in the present tense, and it reflects a goal or behavior that is desired. Now, when Robert hears, "I'm a loser," he changes it to, "I have many skills and am capable of finding a new job." Other affirmations he uses are, "I am getting through this difficult period." and "I am healthy and have a loving family." The list is endless. Think of all the ways you can be creative to change the tape in your mind from a negative to a positive thought. Fill the glass half-full!

What if you see images in your head? What if the thoughts in your head sound like a loud voice? These images and thoughts can haunt you needlessly. Blake's sister was injured in a car accident. He and his sister had a terrible argument the night before her accident. Blake found that the image of the fight continued to invade his mind and cause guilt. He understood intellectually that the fight did not reflect the entirety of their relationship, which was generally good. What could he do? He began by acknowledging that he loved his sister and that it takes two people for a problem to get out of hand and to escalate to a fight. Once he felt secure with the rational explanation, it was important for him to be creative by noticing what was in his mind and then experimenting by changing the thoughts, images, or sounds.

He tried the following techniques: He remembered that his sister was wearing a red dress during the argument. He changed the image of her dress to black and white. When he erased the color, the intensity of his feelings diminished. Any images in color will provoke stronger emotions, whereas black and white will minimize the intensity. Next, he turned down the sound in his mind, as the voices were loud.

Try this yourself. If the voice in your head is too loud pretend you are turning down the volume on a television set. Now, minimize any negative images in your mind and make them microscopic. Project this image outside of your head or onto a wall. If you are remembering the words and they bother you, become a ventriloquist and have them speak to you from another part of your body–from your elbow, your big toe, maybe even your rear end. Did you laugh? You could hear your fight played out in Bugs Bunny's voice.

You could even substitute the phrase "blah-blah-blah", replacing the actual words from the initial fight. Or add soothing music to the scene. Get the picture? Change the picture. Be creative and notice the positive changes.

Experiment and challenge the reality of your thoughts. *Do they serve me? Are they realistic? Exaggerated? Do they add to my life in a positive way or create stress? What would people I respect think of my thoughts? Can I counter negative thoughts with realistic and positive ones?*

Although the variations are limitless, the message is the same. Your feelings will come and go and your loved ones will always be missed, but you have the power to monitor your thoughts and direct them toward healing rather than suffering.

Remember that your energy follows your thoughts and your thoughts determine your behavior and your behavior reflects the quality of your life.

Reinhold Niebuhr sums it up best: "God grant me the serenity to accept the things I cannot change (acceptance), the courage to change the things I can (direct action), and the wisdom to know the difference."

Healing Tears: Nature's medicine drops

❧

Your tears of loss can present you with many scenarios. They can overflow intermittently and without direction, sometimes like a trickling spigot and other times a gushing waterfall. At times you try to hold back this natural expression of grieving. Sometimes it works–other times the choice is not yours, and your body chooses the script. In another situation, you can choose to delay your tears and have them in private.

Sue, a vice President of a corporation, was attending a board meeting shortly after her mother died. As the director of marketing was delivering the annual status report, Sue began to think about her mother and feel weepy. She knew if she cried in front of the board members, it could be political suicide, so she employed a technique in the meeting to keep from feeling her emotions. She used a neurolinguistic technique, looked up with her eyes and not down toward the floor, giving her better control and keeping her composure. It wasn't until she was driving home that the floodgates burst open and Sue was able to feel her overwhelming sadness. The important message is that Sue made a healthy decision. She did not stop her tears but delayed them until she felt comfortable and safe to express them.

Ironically, you can get into deep water and over your head when you choose to stifle your tears. This "fear of the tear" syndrome reflects our Victorian background to appear strong, keep that stiff upper lip, and show little emotion. Coupled with this archetypal pattern is the fear that if you start to cry you may not know how or when the tears will stop. Nothing could be further from the truth.

The next time someone tells you to keep a stiff upper lip and not show those tears, don't listen to them. Tears, in general, especially during the grieving process, will ultimately make you feel better. You will have released a natural load of grief and feel a sense of relief.

Researcher Carl Charnetski, Ph.D., author of **Feeling Good is Good For You: How Pleasure can Boost Your Immune System and Lengthen Your Life** (Carl Charnetski, Francis Brennan, Rodale Press, 2003), says that not all tears are chemically alike. Tears that pour forth when peeling an onion are composed of salt and water, whereas emotional tears contain endorphin-like hormones and proteins that help boost moods and ease anger and pain by aiding in the production of antidepressant chemicals. So a "good cry" indicates that the inherent wisdom of the body is at work, pushing you to release your natural outpouring of sadness and toxins.

How often have you been watching a television program and all of a sudden started to cry? You don't know why–it just happens. It doesn't appear to be connected to anything. Guess again. You may have denied yourself the expression of sadness from previous losses, and at this time, it winds its way out. Feel blessed if you can cry.

Others who stifle their tears can manifest illness or personality difficulties. I am reminded of a client who cried once after the death of his wife and never cried again until five years later when his dog died. He thought that people who cried were weak and an embarrassment, so he put a lid on his tears. This touched off a domino effect and he began to exhibit physical problems that included severe angina, high blood pressure, and depression. His doctor recommended counseling and a stress management program. After a period of two months, he began to understand the proponents of good health and the importance of allowing the natural process of grief to unfold. He cried a great deal in and out of the counseling sessions and eventually, his embarrassment about tears evaporated. He smiles when I ask him what progress he is making. He has even begun to talk to his male friends about learning to express feelings. And with a sparkle in his eyes, he adds that more women are attracted to him since he has become more expressive of his feelings!

His health has improved, his outlook is more positive, and he knows that he will have some difficult days. The next minute can bring a new set of challenges–some sunny, some dark, and some grey. The difference is that he knows he can ride them out. He now thinks of tears as nature's medicine drops that will not drown him–they will bathe him in the relief that he needs to be able to face whatever comes next.

Journaling: Therapy on paper

~

After the death of my brother, I drove to out-of-the-way restaurants and coffee shops, trying to avoid people I knew, wanting to be alone. I would sit for hours and write, surrounded by raw thoughts that seemed to slip off my pen with ease. Days later, I would read what I wrote and wonder whether this depressed soul pouring out her heart was truly me.

I continued to write on a regular basis and realized that, after several weeks, I had compiled quite a rambling of grief. As the losses of loved ones have continued through the years, I have found myself filling many notebooks with my feelings. Through my writing I have begun to realize how my grieving process has changed and how I have begun to have a healthier understanding of the life/death cycle.

James W. Pennebaker, author of **Writing to Heal (New Harbinger Publications-2004)** has conducted ten years of research on the benefits of journaling feelings. His findings demonstrated that those who wrote meaningful journals had a better immune function than those who wrote about superficial subjects. He states that just twenty minutes a day of writing will help ease difficulties and allow you to view your life from a different perspective and may improve your health.

Coping with death or loss and writing about it may bring up strong feelings that can touch off sadness. It is another form of releasing feelings and helping you to process your pain.

The writings will not always make sense or solve the problem of grieving. What they can do is allow you to see the progression of your healing and to witness your journey and growth through the grieving process. So try putting your pen to paper.

Breathing and the Relaxation Response: Grieving's balm

❧

Many years ago, I attended a body/mind Medicine training program that was sponsored by the Body/Mind Institute of the New England Deaconess Hospital and Harvard Medical School in Boston, Massachusetts. Today it is known as the Benson-Henry Institute. The program was instituted in 1988 by Dr. Herbert Benson, cardiologist, Associate Professor of Medicine at Harvard Medical School, author and renowned body/mind researcher. Today, the institute trains clinicians and treats patients from all over the world, teaching them a broad range of self-help and relaxation techniques. People are also educated in areas of nutrition, physical fitness, yoga, breathing, cognitive awareness, and meditation, all geared to improve overall health. Dr. Benson coined the term, "relaxation response," which is the opposite of the fight or flight or stress response. To help us understand how stress affects us and to become aware of its antidote, the relaxation response is key to the program's teachings.

The Body/Mind Institute defines stress as, "the perception of a threat to one's physical or psychological well-being and the perception that one is unable to cope with that threat." The good news, according to Benson and other researchers and teachers, is that, although a person may not be able to alter the stressful situation, he can choose to change the perception of how he thinks about the stress and choose a beneficial response.

The relaxation response can counter the effects of stress by putting you in a deep state of relaxation, thus altering your physiological responses. It is an inborn response and can occur at times when you are not even aware of it, such as when you're relaxing on a beach or listening to soothing music. Essentially, the relaxation response is when metabolism, heart rate, brain rate, blood pressure, breathing rate and muscle tension are all lowered–the opposite of what happens in the stress response.

A certain amount of stress is necessary for our survival and can motivate us to achieve our goals in life. It is when we experience physiological and health changes within our body/mind or spiritual systems that stress works against us and causes us harm.

According to Benson, 60-90 percent of patients who see their primary care physicians present symptoms that are related to lifestyle or stress. The stress response can aggravate diseases, exhaust the adrenal glands, and cause over activity of the sympathetic nervous system. These unhealthy habitual patterns can spill over into our grieving process and make life more difficult during a time when we most need to have a healthy lifestyle.

Many techniques or disciplines can put us in the relaxation response, resulting in positive physiological responses. A few of these are diaphragmatic breathing (belly breathing), meditation, mindfulness (being present to the moment), prayer, yoga, stretching, imagery, progressive muscle relaxation, tai chi, and qigong. Any form of relaxation can help us counter the whirlwinds of the grieving process.

Think of stress-reduction techniques as giving you aid and support through your process of grieving. No matter which relaxation techniques you choose, they may lead to a naturally occurring breathing state. A proverb written by an unknown person says it all. "Life is breath. He who half breathes, half lives." The quality of your breathing process manifests and affects your health, your life, and your grieving process.

Roger Jahnke, doctor of Oriental medicine, author, and qigong master, trains individuals in self-healing techniques. In his book, **The Healing Promise of Qi (McGraw-Hill 2002),** Dr. Jahnke guides you through many sedentary, moving, and breathing exercises that can relieve tension, put you in the relaxation response, and facilitate self-healing.

Jahnke, Dr. Benson, and other health educators describe a common breath known as the essential breath (also called the abdominal breath or yoga breath). This is a breath that can aid healing in general and, particularly soothe you when you are feeling the pain of grief.

Any qualified stress management, yoga, or qigong instructor or any individual trained in breath work can help you to facilitate this on your own. **The Relaxation and Stress Reduction Workbool** (New Harbinger **Publications, 2008**) gives detailed in ing exercises and the relaxation respc

Please remember that it is importa physician before undertaking any b meditation program to ensure there tions to your health.

PART VI

∽

CONCLUSION

The Power of Grieving: A stronger you

The Power of Grieving:
A stronger you

You've been:

- *Recycled through the storms of grief*
- *Brought to your knees and at the same time, forced to stand tall*
- *Isolated in your cave while grasping hungrily for contact*
- *Ripped apart and yet slowly adding one stitch at a time*
- *Gripped so tightly with feelings that they spontaneously burst*
- *Ridden on the waves of hope and despair and gradually noticed some light at the end of the tunnel*

You could not have known that there would be so many surprises and lessons waiting for you along the way.

You have begun to understand that as alone as you are in your grief, you are like every person who has experienced or will experience the death of a loved one. You have begun to understand on a deeper level the ties that bind you to all humanity. There are no borders.

This experience that no one wants to have has been your greatest teacher.

You've learned that:

- *Missing continues forever as life marches on*
- *Letting go of feelings without judgment breeds strength*
- *Tears are necessary and cleansing*
- *Compassion and tolerance have taken on a new meaning*
- *The mystery of life and death will always exist*
- *Your meaning of "strong" has changed*
- *Reaching out to others gives deeper meaning in your purpose to survive*

And most important…you are still here. Here to appreciate the fleeting moment–the moment that can and does bring every type of experience…the moment that always changes…and the moment that can change everything in the blink of an eye.

Yes, your life has changed. You have changed. You can show up in life, a different kind of life. It is the only one you have. The one that you must now "redesign."

PART VII

Losses: The many faces

A Collection of Stories

Losses: The many faces

⁓

Losses are indelibly and flexibly interwoven into the fabric of your life. Every loss resembles a variety of textures–some smooth and others visibly jagged. Like the many fabrics you wear, some losses breathe and recover more easily than others.

The most common loss is death and the one that is most responded to sympathetically. Divorce, the end of a friendship, the loss of a pet, the termination of employment, business dissolution or serious health changes, are among the less acknowledged losses. They are not generally recognized as the difficult passages that they are and yet they can leave you feeling alone without anyone understanding. Many people suffer in silence without support from family or friends.

There are also less identifiable passages that you encounter that can be traumatic in nature and can affect you for a lifetime if you do not find a resolve. These can include unfulfilled love, unrealized lifetime dreams, the loss of a sense of safety, a theft, the loss of freedom of expression or an assault of any kind on our being.

Then there are the losses that reflect the expected developmental stages of life. You could have a change of residence, employment or a change in friendship. Your children leave home, you retire or you segue from youth to aging. In the best selling classic book, **Necessary Losses (Free press-2002)** , Judith Viorst speaks about the journey through these necessary passages of life–the ones that are considered to be normal, the ones everyone experiences. If you do not come to terms with these familiar passages, future losses may bring on more pain and complicate your life.

As difficult as it may be to accept your losses along the way, in the long run, it creates a healthy foundation to move through the rest of what life brings you. By learning to accept losses, you can return to hope and renewal and move beyond. You can tap into the power within you. The following collection of stories is from people who have done just that.

Divorce
Betty Ann

ꙮ

Upon learning of my life partner's desire to begin a "new life," after 35 years, my reaction was a myriad of emotions. There had been a major change in his behavior toward me, but that was said to be because of the stresses of work. This was believable because it had happened before. I tried to bargain and was definitely in denial. I was unable to grasp the concept that he simply didn't love me anymore. Why didn't he ever say it? It might have been easier if he had. It was actually a friend of his who told me this information.

Fear loomed like a leopard ready to pounce at will. I would have to leave the home I thought of as paradise. Find a new place–for one. (I had never been alone in my life). I would have to find a job after having been retired from my field for five years. And, of course, my economic status would change dramatically. I regret that I felt so emotionally depleted, and I could not be a support to my adult children, who were going through their own pain. I was losing our (or were they my?) dreams for the future. Ironically, it would be my life that would change in every way but one.

The good news is…I have wonderful family and friends who were consistently there for me. I had never really been in such need before, and they were truly my support and cheerleaders. I will forever feel that love and return it. I allowed myself to experience all my feelings, and the healing process began. It sounds so simple, but, in fact, it was laden with excruciating pain.

Living alone was very strange initially, not bad…not good. For my entire life, there were always others to take into consideration. Now, I had only myself to consider. My grocery list was different. I left the TV on at night. I stopped making the bed. Small things like this became amazing new discoveries. I discovered that it is not scary being by myself. Yes, sometimes it is lonely, but mostly, it is quite nice. You do what you want when you want.

During the next year, as the divorce process was finalized, I sold my home and found an apartment and job closer to my friends and family. These activities filled a void and were actually a blessing in disguise. Keeping busy is a good thing. And I could actually begin to sense I was on the road to new adventures.

Now, several years later, I can remember the special moments that were a salve to my soul. I began to write in my journal. It became a way to turn some of the obsessive thoughts into poems (I use this word loosely) I treasure today. It felt productive and was very releasing. I did this in front of a blazing fire, sitting in my little wooden rocking chair.

I can't say where I am in the grieving process. But I do know that it gets better and better. I guess I will always miss the good times–and there were many…The family gatherings, the laughter, and my traveling companion. One thing I don't like is the feeling of competition I have with their children's father when it comes to the children at holiday times. I hope that with more time, this too shall pass. It tells me I'm not at the end of this journey yet.

Finally, I have found a way to make some of my dreams come true. I had enough self-confidence this year to leave my job and take advantage of a wonderful opportunity to go around the world. Yes, I did it alone–and met some wonderful people along the way. I have become more aware of my gifts and faults. My own light is beginning to shine.

If I had four words to give to help you through this process, they would be:

FEEL...SUPPORT...WORK...LOVE.

Honoring My Baby
Through Ritual

LaVera

It's been many years since my baby died. He was four days old when he died of a lung infection. Having a baby die is a little-understood loss. Besides the soul connection and holding your child for such a short time, you also lose the dreams of the future you had for your child, and you lose the innocence of life. You lose friends as you grieve a loss so many just don't understand.

What would his voice have sounded like? What would he have looked like? Who would he have been? He is connected with you forever, and he has given you a part of him and taken part of your heart in return, never to be filled by another. It is a shock so hard to comprehend–to move from a joy so great to a sorrow so unforgiving in a matter of blurry moments, then to plunge into grief so deep it's hard to imagine or understand when you had only known this little person for such a short time. How could anyone who has not experienced it, understand it? Even you yourself can't.

To cope with this was very hard. What means do you have? No memories, or very few. An empty nursery that was never used. How do you begin to put your life together?

You begin to heal by letting yourself feel what comes over you, not questioning its validity, weeping when you need to, laughing without guilt when the moment hits you, and making rituals.

I had been making a quilt to bring him home in from the hospital. I had started it at conception, and I had worked on it tirelessly until the trip to the hospital, yet it was still not done. After he died, I tied a knot in my last stitch and put it away while I concentrated on his funeral.

A funeral for a baby? What do you do? What do you say? No one had known him. My husband and I decided to write the whole funeral ourselves. We let each member of our family bless him in their many diverse religions. My husband wrote a song for him. I wrote a song for him. I wrote some special words. We sang lullabies and cried together, then placed the little coffin in the ground. And as we wept, my husband and I covered the little coffin with dirt. My father, who was beside himself seeing me so sad, tried to help, but I needed the completion. It had all happened so fast. I was just trying to find what would make it real.

The months after were still so empty. I conceived again and that brought joy and confusion, guilt and fear. How can I cope with all these emotions? My head spun. Then I decided what would help me. I would finish his quilt. Then I could grieve him in a positive way and love the new child with less guilt. It worked for me. It balanced my emotions and kept me busy, too. When my second and third children were born, they filled my arms that ached so desperately to be filled after my first loss. Life became more joyous. There was still a strange emptiness that left me wondering what I could do to not forget him in our family. So we decided that each year on his birthday we could go for an ice cream cone in his memory. Not so big of a ritual that it will overwhelm or confuse our children, but enough to let them know he will never be forgotten. And enough to let me celebrate my little son, who although his life was short, impacted my life so much, giving me much more understanding, empathy and an appreciation for life and its smallest moments, and for my children, a way of being I may never have had without him.

Life is happy now. I have finally taken the scary leap from grief to memories. I can talk about him without crying. I can laugh without restraint or guilt. Yes, life is good, richer and deeper. I think he rides on my shoulder at times. It's even more colorful. And definitely filled with more love and more time, because now I know what is important.

.

Alone with Multiple Losses

Maggie

∾

"Laugh and the world laughs with you; cry and you cry alone." My mother often repeated this old adage. It took me too many years to understand that it was wrong. I believe that I kept people at a distance with my pretense that everything was just fine; people who were ready to provide me with much needed comfort and emotional support. When you are fragile, however, you are afraid that if you go to the depth of your feelings you will open up an emotional avalanche from which you will never recover. We forget that shared tears do bring us closer to one another and that there is a wonderful camaraderie among people who have traveled to the depth of their pain.

My first deeply felt loss came with the sudden and unexpected death of my closest friend in college. I was propelled into a world of emotional pain unlike any I had known to that point in my life. Those years were filled with other adversities as well but I worked, as I always have, at accepting what life hands me. That is a part of who I am. As it turned out, that time was only a preparation for the life to come.

One year after I married, I was told that my husband had a spinal cord tumor that could not be removed. At the age of 25, Dave became a quadriplegic for the remainder of his life. The loss of having a family of my own was devastating but that became secondary as we struggled with life and Dave started his long journey as a severely disabled man. Grief is usually associated with loss of a person but the loss of the ability of your body to function is an emotional struggle that often surpasses in time and intensity the normal grieving patterns. We joined together in that fight for emotional survival and independence. This was at a time when electric wheelchairs were rare, curb cuts were nonexistent, and the issue of accessible buildings was more than a decade away.

I was my husband's sole caretaker, which included bathing and exercising him, dressing and feeding him, brushing his teeth and evacuating his bowels. I became his arms, hands and legs for he eventually, against all odds at that time, began to practice law. I was also the object of his anger and frustration as he raged against his disability and what had happened to him. We were rarely apart, and when we were, I was anxious to be home for I lived in fear that something would happen while I was gone–that he would lose his balance in his chair or that his bladder would be full and I would come home to a proud and angry man who had wet his pants. The intensity of our lives and the constant companionship forced us to always communicate and address issues that were breaking our hearts and our spirits. And during all of this, I remembered my first lesson in grief: what it feels like to lose someone you love. For all of its pain, grief is a great teacher.

Dave's death was sudden after 18 years of marriage. Initially, there was the numbness but worse than that were those brief times when I felt I was among the walking dead.

The emotional roller coaster ride that follows is preferable. There were good days and I took advantage of them for I never knew what the next day would bring to my day-to-day existence. My husband's death brought me a freedom and an exhilaration that I could not or would not discuss with others. This was coupled with tremendous sadness and the loss of a close companionship forged by the very adversities that made life so difficult. I functioned quite well given the circumstances because I had also learned back in college that life does go on and that time does heal. I was becoming quite an expert on grief now, a practiced hand at it—or at least that is what I thought. Truthfully, though, my ability to function was also based upon my stifling of the enormity of my loss and the abrupt and devastating change in my life.

The emotional pain and feeling of aloneness increased with time, especially as I struggled with the infirmity of my elderly parents. As I approached my 50th birthday, I was diagnosed with Chronic Lymphocytic Leukemia. On the surface, I appeared to have accepted this one more setback, but I was becoming angry; it was more difficult to concentrate on work. I realized that I did not laugh as I once did and it had been my slightly skewed sense of humor that helped me through the tough times. I needed to move forward for I was wasting what now may be valuable time. For the first time in my life, I consulted a therapist and I was able to voice the unspoken and unaddressed pain. It is so easy to slip unknowingly into a state of mind that one mistakes for the way things have to be.

How I manifested grief was learned from others. I was brought up by a generation of people who did not share or even show their feelings; who loved but could not demonstrate that love. When I lost my roommate in college, my pain was raw and evident. I was told that my grief was excessive by people who should have known better. As I became more responsible with age, I realized that there is always someone else to think about, to care for, to distract you when a loss occurs. My husband became paralyzed from the chest down. There was so much to do; I will cry later. Then he died. Shock numbs my mind to protect my soul; I will grieve when I am stronger. My much-loved father slipped into dementia and then into death. My mother had such need of me. I will mourn another time. Two years later my mother gave up the struggle and died. I then had the energy and perhaps the courage to grieve but there is a time for joy and a time for mourning and those of us who can't get that timing down feel a bit out of sync.

Today, I am without parent or sibling, child, spouse or significant other. The loss of both parents left me with a feeling of utter aloneness that I neither expected nor imagined because I thought I had prepared myself. You can't. Seeing one sister put an arm around another at a wedding was enough to send me unexpectedly spiraling from a sense of well being into excruciating pain. Sitting at another wedding surrounded by couples careened me into the dark of the outside night where I spent the next couple of hours walking and wandering alone in an attempt to control my pain and my tears. These episodes were like unexpected volcanic eruptions. They came, I believe, because I was unable to mourn and shed all my tears when I needed to. You have to have the courage to look at your loss full in the face and give it its due before you can travel forward. There is no right way to do it and each grief is different from the one before. It must be done if we are to reinvest in life.

The difficult times have helped me cherish the friends and family that I have for I realize, more fully than some, that our time together is precious. My personal and professional relationships have been enhanced by a knowledge and understanding of those who have suffered and I am thankful for that. Having traveled to the depth of my pain I continue to grow and find peace in my aloneness. I feel whole again and can more easily open myself to others. I have survived and face the future with the anticipation that I will be able to meet the obstacles ahead for I have learned how to live and live well in spite of adversity.

The Loss of a Child

Fran

∾

Our daughter, Teresa Ann Churilla, (Terri), was a bright, bubbly, outgoing nineteen year old dedicated to academics, and very active in school and extra curricular activities. In high school she won many prestigious awards, was editor of the school newspaper and yearbook, a member of the drama club, a cheerleader and Salutatorian of her class. In college, Terri was a bio pre-med major, a member of the ski club, Eucharist minister, and on the Dean's List. She loved helping others and always wore a smile.

At 19, Terri was killed in a skiing accident. This tragedy left me in shock for about a year, but I kept busy organizing newspaper articles, writing thank you notes and establishing a scholarship in Terri's memory. Then the anger and depression set in and all I did was cry. I couldn't concentrate, couldn't put an outfit together or go to the grocery store.

At one point, my daughter Tracy screamed at me, "You know you still have me!" This jolted me and I called a clinical psychologist, Teresa Rando, who specialized in grieving. I spent five years crying and experiencing a gamut of feelings. The second year was worse than the first and definitely, the worst of my life.

One day, a woman name Joan, who saw Terri's obituary phoned me. Joan's only child had died and she said her son was so much like Terri. Another woman who played tennis next to me said her son died at age eighteen in a skiing accident. Our "Good Grief" group soon grew from three to twenty-one and we met monthly to support one another. All the talking and sharing of our feelings was key to my recovery.

Because of my loving husband and daughter, I knew I had to get through this and give myself back to them. My wonderful therapist, caring friends, my faith in God and St.

Teresa, talking and feeling, slowly got me back to some faith in continuing on. To this day, I have eight friends who will speak openly about our beloved Terri. For these friends, I am most thankful! I also have anniversary masses said twice a year and publish a memoriam every five years. This is a helping ritual.

Through all this I have learned how precious life is. I urge parents to love their children dearly and live each day to the fullest. I am so happy we had given Terri as much as we did. For grieving parents, use these tools to help relieve your pain. My heart goes out to you.

Finding Meaning
Andrew

∾

The grace I found from the death of my mom was in her, how beautiful she still was even after dying in front of my eyes. She had not eaten for almost three weeks and was so thin from the cancer, yet her face had such beauty, as though no disease could ever take that away. When the moment arrived that I had feared for so long, incredibly, I was so comfortable lying with my arms around her for a while, still realizing how much she meant to me.

Spending years fighting cancer with my mom and slowly losing her taught me so much about appreciating life and every day we have with our health. That's the basic lesson that changed my thinking from what she taught me: "If you have your health, you have everything." All the other pieces of life fall into place after that because when your health is in jeopardy, nothing else matters. Stressing about finances, jobs, relationships, or any part of our daily lives seems irrelevant when a serious health risk arises. Until it happens to you or someone very close to you, it's a difficult concept to grasp, but for me, it completely changed my life.

Sounds like I dealt with it all so smoothly, but actually I didn't.–It took me over two years to come to terms with my mom's death and come out of my shell of depression. These days I only think about the happy, joyful times we had together and how lucky I was to have had such a great relationship with her. (I meet far too many people who take their parents for granted or don't get along with them). She taught me so many lessons about life and how important family is–concepts that I had a hard time grasping at the time but now understand clearly. This is where my spiritual approach to life comes from–believing first in yourself and what's in your heart and appreciating life to the fullest. Don't take health for granted, because nothing else will matter if all of a sudden an illness strikes. Occasionally, when I forget these things and am stressing about something ridiculous, I'll stop and realize that I have my health, family, food, clothes and shelter, so just enjoy the day as much as possible and try to make it special.

Saying Goodbye
to a Child
Cynthia

∾

The hardest goodbye of all is for a mom to place a child into adoption. Making the decision to place a child in adoption and saying goodbye is one of the most difficult things a mother can ever do. A tremendous amount of attention is paid to the separation and loss issues that adoptees may have because of initial separations from their birth moms either during infancy or later in their childhood through the child welfare system. The importance of saying goodbye, developing life books and supporting children is essential and well documented.

I worked with many children and moms over the years to help them make the best decisions for their children. If the decision was to place the child in adoption, I also facilitated goodbyes between moms and young children or older children who had been in foster care and moved into adoption.

This is very difficult and painful for everyone involved in the process. It is important to help develop a life book that has much information about the parents and the reason for the decision. To do this, you need to reach out to the birth family and provide the support they need. I have never met a birth parent who did not love his child and wish that the placement was not necessary. Many moms and dads have wished with all their hearts that this goodbye would not have to happen. Some were able to keep in contact, while for others, it was not possible. Parents are making good decisions for their child and need all the support they can get. Most people cannot imagine how this could happen and are likely to blame the parents and assume the worst about them.

Usually parents in this situation have no friends or family that they can turn to for support. Often they are judged and blamed for a decision that is done out of love. It is essential that these birth parents be provided empathy and support. They need to know that they have made the best decision for the child and situation. They need to be valued as full partners in the decision and relied upon to help as much as possible with developing the life book for the child to take with them.

Some of the best transitions for a child have been gradual, with the birth parent as well as the adoptive parent participating and providing all the transitions needed for the child's developmental age. It is much more difficult for birth and adoptive parents to go through this process. It brings up tremendous feelings and pain in all parties and often adults would like to rush through this and "get it over with." Not all parents are able to go through a gradual transition, and if it is too much, they should not, because it will not be the productive experience a child needs.

The bravest moms I ever met worked together and provided a transition for a very young boy and then, later, his two sisters, who moved in with the same family. She knew that it was best for the children. No one in her family and none of her friends understood why she was doing this, and she did not have emotional support from any of them. At first, she did not want to go to the adoptive home. She felt that mom was "a better person" than she, and she blamed herself a great deal for being in this situation. The adoptive mom had a hard time imagining a mom doing this and it brought up many feelings of loss to go through it. Both moms said it would be easier for them to have a very quick transition and avoid the feelings as much as possible. They both, however, were able to put their own needs aside and make a plan to put the needs of the children first. Two very strong and insightful moms worked together with social workers to make the best plan possible for the siblings.

On the final day of goodbyes, we also had a ceremony of lighting candles to represent the love that was lit within the children's hearts and would always stay with them. I remember joining the moms and children in their sadness and grief to say their goodbyes. The birth mom was key in giving the children permission to attach to their new family. Her permission and presence in working with the new mom gave the children a sense of safety and allowed them to make attachments more easily to their new family. It was very painful and hard for the birth mom to do this and also hard for the adoptive mom to see. There is no way to participate in this transition without sharing the pain and grief. Any loss triggers feelings and experiences of loss in each person's life. It is very tempting to avoid and ignore these feelings, but all change brings them up, whether one is aware of them or not.

It is a beautiful thing to help a child attach to a new family. The stage is set for positive development and the encouragement to flourish. It is also key to help moms feel the importance and value they have had in a child's transition and feel some closure so they can also move on with their own lives. Birth moms need to know how valuable their help has been in transitioning children to a new family and that they have done their very best. They need to be validated and recognized for their significance and contribution to the child's future happiness. Birth moms need to be helped through their pain and supported through their own grieving process.

Evaporated Dreams
Gwen

∽

I was 37 years old when I lost my mother. I had just gotten married four months earlier. All the dreams of sharing my new life with her were now gone. I realized that I would never share what I've come to know as the joy of motherhood. All that I never imagined could happen so early in my life was now a reality.

I remember the day I received the devastating news that my mother had a fatal form of lung cancer. I had just returned home from my honeymoon to the phone call that shook my world. "Mom has oat cell cancer," which I later learned was a rapidly growing cancer. The prognosis was not good.

My reaction was one of pure panic. I began to tremble. How was I going to live without her? Whom would I talk to about the many things so close to my heart? I called cancer centers to talk to anyone who would listen. I went to New Age stores and bought books and tapes that I hoped could help her visualize her cancer away.

I remember feeling deep inside that somehow I had to save her, but I came to realize that I could not. This was her journey, and in the end, she would have to face her life herself. I realized that someday this would also be my challenge.

As the disease progressed, between the morphine and the devastating effects of her one chemotherapy treatment, I saw my mother begin to fade away from me. She slept much of the time, and the reality of not having her here began to hit me emotionally. Things got worse when mom had a stroke. As I sat bedside her and prayed and prayed for her not to die, I took her hand and kissed her face. She heard me weep and said in her garbled voice, "My diamond, my diamond, please don't cry." Those words were a gift I would later savor.

She slipped into a coma. At this time, I decided to talk to her. *I believe the following events were cosmically orchestrated.* I began to tell her that she had been a good wife and mother and that she didn't need to suffer anymore and that everyone she loved who had passed on would be waiting for her. With this, her breathing began to change rapidly, shallow and panting. In the room with me were a nurse and her aide. The aide put his arms around my waist to support me, as my knees were beginning to buckle. He assured me, "It's O.K. honey, just let her go." " I love you, mom," I said. She opened her eyes, took one last look at me and drew her last breaths. Another gift I could savor in the future. I sat next to her marble-like body, in some kind of awe as to what had just transpired. This was it. This was the end of my mother and me. Did this really happen? No, it couldn't have–but it did. It took a really long time to process this. After several years of what seemed to be endless crying, panic attacks and just gut-wrenching pain about her troubled life, I began to emerge from my grief.

Three years later, after my beautiful daughter was born, I would look into her huge brown eyes, like my mother's, and realize that my mother would never be gone in my heart, that every day my daughter is a reminder to me of

Mom and also of what we shared together, both good and bad.

I have learned to face some of my own fears about death and dying. I remember her words: "Life is short, Gwen, do good things for yourself." I try to remember these words every day. My life was enriched by being with her at the end. The moments we shared were some of the hardest and most tender moments I've ever known. I carry them with me daily.

Forgiving a Parent
David

～

"Honor thy mother and father." I never really understood this commandment until I began to work through my mother's death. It's very easy for a child (especially as an adult) to love and respect a parent who loves and cares for him unconditionally. Returning this love comes naturally to the child. But for the parent who has had difficulties giving unconditional love and care, the child becomes challenged spiritually. For that child must now understand that to honor his mother or father, that child will have to learn how to forgive.

Simply put, God wants us to learn how to forgive. If we learn this important tenet we will elevate ourselves spiritually. And what greater challenge can there be for a child than to forgive a parent who has, for whatever reason, brought unnecessary pain into that child's life?

Five years after my mother's death, I can say I've learned to forgive her for my unnecessary pain. It has taken me time to achieve this, and I am certain that her illness cleared the way for this healing process. When you are saying goodbye, you realize you have limited time. For those who have lost a loved one to a sudden death, the opportunity is often lost. So if you have the time, use it to forgive.

My wife, Limor, encouraged me to talk to my mother while she was alive. Limor, who was born and raised in Israel, had a hard time understanding why many families in America prefer to share their feelings in therapy with a stranger as opposed to speaking with the person they had issues with in their family. Having lived in Israel for a year during the last two years of my mother's life, I began to realize the importance of direct communication with family and friends. So with my wife's support, I spent much time talking with my mom towards the end of her life.

Throughout the later stages of her battle with cancer, I was allowed time to empty my heart of the hurts that I had carried around since childhood–feelings I never felt confident to share with mom. And she listened. This was a beautiful aspect of her personality. Not every parent is willing to face this type of pain. And this allowed me to heal. I believe a dying parent can truly help their child by just listening, being open to forgiveness.

Mom died between the high holidays of Rosh Hashanah and Yom Kippur. I'll never forget how hard it was to pick myself up off the couch and walk to synagogue to recite Kaddish (a prayer for the dead) after her death. It was as though a massive weight lay on me, restraining and coaxing me to stay down and surrender. Thank God, I made the walk to the synagogue. You need to move physically at such times. It helped me to release many feelings that helped me to heal.

When I daydream now, I can recall the bright colors of my mother's living room. A memory of light pastels and warm strings of sun. These are the colors of life and forgiveness. I miss mom. I light a candle and say Kaddish in synagogue. All to honor her, and me, and life.

Loss of Country
Adriana

◟

I arrived in Hartford, Connecticut, from Santiago, Chile in April 1974. It was almost six months after the military coup put an end to the democratically elected government of Chilean President Salvador Allende on September 11, 1973. It was a cold and snowy April day. It mirrored the desolation in my heart. I had left both my parents and five brothers and sisters and their families in search of safety from one of the most brutal dictatorships in Latin America. As I walked facing the cold wind, tears ran down my cheeks. It would take weeks and months for me to feel safe from the nightly excursions of the military trucks driving the streets of Santiago during the curfew, knocking on doors and taking prisoners, many of who were never seen again.

I had been the Chair of the Urban Department of the School of Social Work of the Catholic University. Shortly after the coup, the new administration at the university terminated the contracts of about sixty percent of the faculty and administration at our school. Community organizing, group work, rural and urban departments were eliminated. Casework was the only method allowed.

A few weeks later, while at home with a colleague, we heard knocks at the door. I opened it and found myself in front of an armed group of the military police. They asked for me, pushed their way in to search the apartment, turned beds upside down, broke open a locked winter clothes chest with the butt of a rifle and seized books and records. I was led out to a police jeep and taken to a police station where I went through my first interrogation. From there, I was taken to a cell in the headquarters of the Chilean Bureau of Investigations.

I was in the company of many "companeras" in a tiny and dark cell from which we could hear the screams and cries of prisoners who were being interrogated and tortured. Two men were my interrogators. Blindfolded, I could not see their faces, only hear their voices. They were seeking names of the supporters of the Allende government with whom I had done political work. I was stripped from the waist up and threatened with electricity. Somehow, I kept calm and refused to give any names, arguing with them without raising my voice. I appealed to them as persons, members of a family, suggesting how they would feel if their mother, wife, daughter or sister were being treated as I was. I was asked to sign without being allowed to read or see what I was signing and was given my clothes back and told to go back to the cell. The following morning, I was told I could go on home arrest. My home was watched, which prevented my friends from visiting. A month later, I was told I was free to go. It was thanks to the solidarity of a group of women, members of the League of Women Voters, that I was given the opportunity to start a new life in Connecticut where I now reside.

As I look back, I try to relive the feelings and recall how I survived those months in Chile. The prevailing feeling during the dictatorship was one of helplessness. It was hard to conceive and realize that all legal protection was gone. New edicts substituted for Chile's long-established rule of the law. During my detention, I went into my head. I could not allow myself to feel. That time would come. I had to think how not to succumb to fear or desperation. During my month of home arrest, when I sewed my only handmade blouse while at home alone, there was more anger than tears in my heart. I feared, aware of the power that the men in uniform had over each one of us civilians, for my safety and that of those I knew and loved. But I was mostly outraged that our efforts to establish a more just and equitable democracy had come to this.

During those first few months in Hartford, I finally cried for the loss of family, friends and homeland. My grief was delayed for the purpose of survival. The sense of loss lessened as I focused on my research work with a local Latino nonprofit group. As I have discovered over time, work is great medicine.

Other learnings include appreciation for the generosity of individuals and groups that welcomed and supported me over those difficult months. These include urban and suburban, Latino, African-American and Caucasian. I learned to rely on others and to accept the selfless gift of their friendship. I also got to know myself better and realized that I could not get through life alone, but I finally could move on through work, solidarity, getting involved with the local community, the closeness and connection of others, and starting a new home and family.

Life is stronger than our worst fears and greatest joys.

Healing Through Dreams
Rita

∾

Shortly before his death, my dear friend, Paul, entrusted to me his treasured meditation music. He had carefully selected the hauntingly beautiful pieces over the ten years of his remarkable spiritual journey from a CEO living in Westchester County, New York, to life in India, where he studied and practiced Eastern religions. Paul returned to the states enlightened and spent five years composing his book on cosmology. I came to meet Paul serendipitously, the day after watching a library video of a discussion among physicists on the nature of the universe. Paul and I very quickly eased into a deep discourse and kinship.

The bond that developed between us seemed to have a mystical component. Several months into the relationship, I had a dream in which a tribal council meeting was being held in a large tent around a long oval table. Paul was the Holy Man/Chief who sat at the head conducting the meeting. I was moving about serving the seated men. Paul suddenly stopped the meeting, motioned with his right arm for the men to move down, and then beckoned me to come and sit next to him on his right side. He then looked me fully in the face with great love, held the gaze for a long time, tapped my shoulder and then tapped the sacred tablets he was holding up in his hand. He looked at me and said, "For you. For you," as he tapped the tablets.

After Paul was diagnosed with terminal cancer, he asked me one evening to prepare his will, with instructions for his funeral and loving messages for his family and friends. He was not afraid to die. He could see beyond mortal existence and the clutches of duality (pleasure/pain, good/evil).

Paul's dictated dying wishes were beautifully carried out on a bright, frigid January afternoon along the Charles River in Cambridge. We read passages from the Bhagavad-Gita, from the Bible and from Paul's book. With his favorite meditation music playing, his ashes were scattered into the river along with rose petals. They spread outward, and as they were carried along in the current, I felt a deep inner peace. I could feel his presence and pleasure at our loving tribute to him.

The spiritual power of this extraordinary man survived his bodily death. Three months later, on a Sunday afternoon, with sun streaming onto the living room couch, I lay back, turned on Paul's music and drifted into the most delicious sleep. In my dream I gave birth to a third child, a daughter. When I picked her up and looked into her face I saw the most radiantly beautiful little girl. I realized with absolute certainty that she had within her a special spiritual calling–like the Dalai Lama. I recognized that it was critically important that she be reared with exquisite tenderness and care. I knew it was imperative that I treasure, and allow to flourish, this special gift my baby had. Upon awakening, I felt that Paul had sent me that dream as a reminder, and that the baby was myself.

Burying Feelings
Hank

∽

When I was 20 years old, my father died suddenly of a heart attack. We had a very close relationship, and I became frightened that I wouldn't be able to cope with losing him. For the first time in my life, I felt that I was facing a situation I wouldn't be able to handle. Within a couple of days, I made a conscious decision to stop crying and feeling sorry for myself. With that decision, I short-circuited my grieving process and resolved to be strong. When I went to the funeral, I wanted to show my relatives that I was OK, so I smiled when I greeted them. I tried to concentrate on how fortunate I was to have had him all of my then-short life.

In shutting down my feelings of pain, I didn't realize at the time that I was also shutting down my ability to feel joy as well. It was not that I went into a depression. Looking back, I could have felt more happiness in other areas had I allowed myself to feel the pain, but it was too scary.

I eventually grieved his loss at a workshop that was not only spiritual but also practical in that it stepped me through reliving how much I loved him and missed him. The tears were real, and I felt safe in this supportive environment. I realized from this process how important it is to allow whatever I'm feeling to come up and just experience the feeling. I learned that I am more alive by doing this than by suppressing what I'm feeling.

I would advise everyone to get support during their grieving, either through a professional or friends, and be aware that grieving is a process that not only helps to resolve the pain but can bring one to a place where they're stronger than before.

Surviving Death and Trauma at an Early Age

Marie

∽

It was a hot August morning three weeks before school started. Over the weekend my mother had asked my father to leave. The lies, the affairs, the constant moving, the fighting, and the incredible dysfunction that existed could no longer be tolerated by my mother. She made me feel safe throughout it all. That hot Monday morning changed everything. My mother had a heart attack in front of my eight-year-old sister and me. When my mother was having her second heart attack moments later, she asked me to take care of my sister. The ambulance took my mother to the hospital. She died four days later.

My innocence was immediately taken from me and I had no idea what I would experience over the next few days since I had never been to a funeral before. From that moment on, our lives were beyond chaotic and painful. My teen years were taken from me without warning. I was faced with making adult decisions the moment my mother died. My father suffered from manic depression and went untreated until the day he died. I was suddenly self-parenting and at the same time being a parent to my sister and often, to my father. I was *unable to* grieve for my mother. I felt if I went to that very painful place I would fall apart.

For many years, my growth was stunted by verbal abuse. During my teenage years we continued moving from apartment to apartment (we had moved fifteen times in fifteen years). We were without heat and hot water, electricity and without a car from time to time. I was always frightened and uncertain. Sometimes my father would wake me in the middle of the night and tell me he needed two hundred and fifty dollars by tomorrow or our electricity would be shut off. I was fifteen and terrified. My sister's illness surfaced several months after my mother's death. I was unaware that I was surrounded by manic depression but was now convinced I was to blame for the erratic behavior that surrounded me.

Life continued to be difficult. In my twenties, I was a bitter, sorrowful, young woman and would pray that I was older so my pain would not stab me every moment of every day. During that era I made a lot of mistakes hurting others and sometimes myself along the way. I judged men by the fact that if they had two parents that seemed normal and a mother who was kind to me then they were perfect for me. This did not end up working.

My life continued to be painful. My father died when I was thirty-five and I had still not grieved my mother's death and all my childhood losses. A multitude of problems finally led me to seek counseling.

Today I am in my fifties and my feelings are still raw at times. Yet with the help of a therapist, I grieved and learned much about my self. I learned I was not to blame for anything that happened. There are still emotions that I have to learn to live with, as some scars never go away. The difference today is that I take a positive approach to life and am grateful for everything that comes my way. Everything is a learning experience and I have learned many lessons about life. These lessons have taught me how to love and how to open my heart to all those who cross my path. My pain connects me to all humanity as does my love. Today I share a wonderful life with my husband, pets, my dear sister, and brother-in-law, in addition to special friends who are my extended family.

Whatcom Creek–A Human and Ecological Disaster

Bruce

❧

When I first walked along Whatcom Creek, I knew that Bellingham, Washington had something unique. Despite years of damage and neglect, the heart of the creek was still alive. There was potential to extend that life throughout the watershed. Whatcom Creek had the potential to be a healthy, lively and evolving salmon-bearing stream running right through the heart of downtown Bellingham. To make it happen would take years of work and a strong commitment from the whole community. I knew right then and there that I wanted to make it happen. As an environmental specialist IV for the State of Washington, I took on the challenge. Whatcom Creek was hope for a future in which both people and natural systems thrived. Through hard work, volunteers, research and endless hours, the process began.

A federal grant helped purchase land along Whatcom Creek to create "Salmon Park–A Park for Salmon." The Rotary Club built a fish ladder over an old sewer line crossing that allowed Chinook salmon to spawn in the gravels of upper Whatcom for the first time in over one hundred years. Volunteers planted the barren banks of lower Whatcom Creek with indigenous plants that would eventually provide shade and stabilize bank erosion.

After five years of effort it was beginning to work. Life was returning to Whatcom Creek. There were one-and two-year old baby Chinook surviving, living in Whatcom Creek, in downtown Bellingham. Again we sampled the biology of the streams and were surprised at the health of the Salmon Park area. Species of long-lived aquatic insects you would expect to find only in cold-water mountain streams were thriving in Whatcom Creek.

The good news kept coming. Georgia-Pacific shut down its elemental chlorine plant– eliminating ongoing mercury contamination. Businesses captured their run-off, recycled their waste and crushed their oil filters. Residents reduced their use of pesticides, picked up dog waste and composted more.

Many, many small actions by the Whatcom Creek community began to sing with one small voice that grew to a choir praising the salmon's return. If we could do it here in Bellingham, it could happen everywhere. And we were doing it.

On June 10, 1999. Whatcom Creek was gone. An explosion of gasoline, jet fuel and diesel pipeline from the nearby ARCO refinery ruptured underground, spilling 275,000 gallons of diesel gasoline into Whatcom Creek. The gasoline flowed into Whatcom Falls Park and filled the canyon with vapors, killing an 18-year-old boy who was fishing. He was overcome by the blanket of fumes, fell into the creek and drowned. Two nine-year-old boys (one a friend of my son Luke) were walking along a trail in the park, clicking a lighter, and suddenly ignited a 2-mile-long, 1,000-foot-high explosion and fireball. This human tragedy of young people dying is still impossible to comprehend and will take a lifetime to understand and heal.

The fire had evaporated the creek and flowed flaming gasoline, killing everything that lived in or near the creek. Thousands of dead animals.

I was in shock, and numbed for days. I still had to do my job. Every day for months, I gathered dead critters to quantify damages, planned emergency response and how to remediate gasoline imbedded in the creek in time for returning spawning salmon.

Every morning seemed to bring extra weight until about eleven months later I couldn't carry it anymore. I became more and more emotional, crying easily, sleeping less and less. I sought counseling. After two visits, the counselor insisted that I get out of any work involving the creek. After another two visits my counselor used a technique called Thought Field therapy to take the images burning in front of my mind's eye and send them to the background where I could choose to see them or not. She then broke it to me that I was clinically depressed and that I needed to take three or four months off and be on medication. I saw a psychologist, and he prescribed antidepressants.

It has been several years since the explosion, and I'm still processing feelings and investing more in life. The work of recovery from what I've come to see as a crisis of the spirit continues. I wept twice writing this piece. I have found that grief takes tremendous energy, but it takes even more energy to avoid it. I feel that if I had not been dedicated to repairing the creek, hadn't listened to my own pain, and hadn't had the courage to "stop the world and take care of myself," more damage would have been done. Now, when the wave of grief tries to carry me away, I find a way to let it gently lift me from my focus and quietly set me back on the ground. The waves have become smaller and smaller, but I have a sense that they will always be there.

What has helped me the most are counseling and the Thought Field Therapy. They turned me away from the path of denial and trapped energy. The medications numbed me in many ways for over a year, and I am not sure that they helped the process beyond slowing it down. Having loving support from my wife, family, boss and office mates kept me going.

There are many positive learnings that have come out of this tragedy. I have new directions in my work. I am now working, as part of my job, to bring biodiesel products to the Pacific Northwest. "Salmon Park," a park for salmon and people in downtown Bellingham, has grown from five acres to over one hundred acres. I had started writing a book before the blast. The process of writing became more difficult but fruitful, and I have recently published my first book. I now have a deeper understanding and respect for grief and the grieving process. I can see it in other people now and have become more compassionate.

Some of the lessons I have learned include: Listen carefully to those who love you and share with them your deepest feelings. Take action to stop the damage by getting help as soon as possible to begin the repair. Know that you need to let go and even though it doesn't feel like it, that you will survive. Let the tidal waves of grief lift and hurl you through curtains of uncertain turmoil. You have to; if you don't, the waves only get larger. Also, above all else, know you will survive and be stronger for it. I'm not sure if, over time, the waves of grief get smaller, or if I simply get better at seeing them coming and riding them out.

Learnings from Care Giving

Anita

∾

The pain is always there. Filed away in the Rolodex of my brain when I experience grief or joy the sense of loss reappears. That pain was present when Paige Lieberman Chestler entered this world but Paula Lieberman did not bear witness to the birth of her first grandchild.

How do you prepare for the death of your friend? There is no plan, no course of action. You are guided by instinct and dive in–and then the plan evolves. Paula was diagnosed with cancer and as her dear friend, I decided to put my life on hold. Along with other friends, we were determined to take control of the disease. Women know how to bond. We had a common goal. Suddenly, Paula's friends became mine.

As the cancer progressed so did the friendships. Honesty was not an option with Paula but mandatory! We researched wigs and knew everything about her treatments. I was obsessed with spending time with Paula–there was never enough in the end. With great sadness comes wonderful humor made necessary by the tragedy. Paula returned to the hospital on an emergency basis. Barbara and

I were her escorts. Paula looked well in her Uma Thurman wig. Barbara walked with a cane as I tried to fight a pounding headache. The nurse scrutinized the three of us and questioned, "Which one is the patient?" Tears of laughter streamed down our cheeks!

Paula touched her friends and family with her honesty, values, love and ability to live life to the fullest. She has changed my life for the better. She taught me to be strong, by example. I now understand the vital part true friendships play in one's life.

As I navigated (and still do) my way through the grieving process, I realized my family and friends are the center of my universe. Nothing brings you more joy or pain than relationships. The strength of friendships and the love of family enable you to survive.

Today, many years later, I smile, am thankful and cherish the moments I had with Paula rather than focus on what I lost.

Ritual as Healing

Loretta

∾

Several years ago, a friend of mine, who was a foster mother, adopted one of her foster children, who was one of a set of triplets, in her late teens and had a long psychiatric history. She had struggled with major mental health issues in addition to her difficulties in her natural family. She had periods of time when she was able to function quite well, was able to work, related to her sisters, and had a boyfriend. On other occasions, she became withdrawn, depressed, frightened and despairing. On one of these occasions, she committed suicide.

My friend asked me to do some sort of ritual as a memorial service for this young woman. At first, several of her friends were nervous about getting together, as everyone was having trouble dealing with what had happened. I felt it would be important to have people share their feelings about how this woman had died before any healing could occur. As they began to share their anger, confusion, fear and disbelief, everyone was listening and the whole energy in the room changed. Sadness and grief were mixed with all sorts of humorous and tender experiences that people had shared with this young woman. Some talked about how hard it was to accept their feelings of anger, because they felt they should be feeling sad. Some expressed guilt that they should have been more supportive to her. Many expressed that they had been hesitant and fearful prior to attending the ritual, but having come, they were glad to have the opportunity to share memories of their friend. I was impressed that after expressing feelings of rage and guilt, people were able to move into sadness, memories and acceptance. I was moved by the power that sharing a common feeling in a group and learning of similar reactions and feelings had on the healing experience.

Abuse and Loss of
Dreams
Natalie

⟳

ME NATALIE, possessing the audacity to speak of wholeness, even the possibility of it. All my inner critics, judges and saboteurs of my joy and greatness squirm pathetically.

How dare she speak of it, voice it, as a possibility? All of this stuck in my psyche that becomes my life.

What is happening to us?

Fighting, screaming, dramatics played out somewhere in my life. Screw ups, seething tentacles reaching for hopelessness, disasters, disillusionment, pity, self-recrimination and, oh yes, SHAME.

How dare she even speak the words wholeness, integration. Ha! They laugh.

She will never know it. Little whispers arise.

Yes, look how far she has come…abuse, bulimia, rape, incest, abandonment, alienation, self-induced failures, losses, and loss of dreams.

Do you think she could win?

No! We cannot allow it.

We would disappear only to rear up in extreme conditions. Like the wicked witch....

What will show up? Can we melt? Can we heal?

Out of the ashes of doubt, fear and longing comes tenacity.
I have worked so hard.
Countless hours of dreaming, journaling, dancing,
        counseling, workshops, yoga, movement therapy.
Always learning, growing, trying.

I am rising from the ashes.
Moment by moment the sun arises from my pain.
Beauty upon beauty surfacing, mountainous, unshakable
        essence of truth and spontaneity.
All faucets turned on.
Creativity, imagination, laughter, beauty, passion, anger.
Willingness to go deep.

A voice as clear as the ocean.
Riding, changing, flowing in each moment.
Within a container strong, bendable, pliable, fluid, rooted.
Connectedness.
Continually healing from my losses. Connectedness felt
        and true.
ME, Natalie, here, hopeful and whole.
NOW...YES.

Sufferings from the Chinese Revolution, "My Lotus Grown Out of Mud"

Lijun Cheng

∽

In 1966, a movement called the Great Cultural Revolution blew through the Chinese society like an intense storm. Wearing army clothes and waving Mao's "Little Red Book", the Red Guard created a state of anarchy. I was swept up in the storm and lost my freedom for eighteen years because I was labeled a counter-revolutionary. Simple things were interpreted as crimes–a note written to a friend, a letter written to my parents, entries in my diary. They would take a word I'd written out of context and use that as proof that I was against Mao and the Cultural Revolution. I'd say. "I'm not against Mao. Understand my whole intent." I refused to admit to crimes I had not committed. My refusal was interpreted as having a bad attitude and that was considered a crime. They said I was a class enemy and beat me.

Everything in my life was controlled. I was incarcerated in a small room at my workplace for six months. I didn't know where my husband and children were. I was targeted in many struggle meetings where I had to stand on a stool wearing a tall paper hat while being beaten and humiliated–often with my young son and daughter being forced to watch. I was captured several times by mobs that beat me nearly to the point of death. I was assigned to perform heavy labor in a farm village where intellectuals and office workers were being educated by learning the ways of the farmers. I was watched constantly even when I had to use the bathroom.

The physical suffering is only part of the story. I was much more tortured mentally. It hurt me deeply that people who didn't know me would participate in humiliating me. I had little human warmth or love for eighteen years. I dared not approach friends or family because I would put them in jeopardy because I still carried "the hat" of the anti-revolutionary label and was constantly under surveillance by the government.

In 1984, the government investigated my case and admitted that the way I was treated was a miscarriage of justice. This admission was publicized in Bejing in every major newspaper and announced on every radio station. I regained my reputation and was promoted to a job in the central government. Regaining my reputation means a great deal to me. Once the dangerous "class enemy" label was lifted friends and neighbors poured into my home.

My body was seriously damaged during the Cultural Revolution. Some of the damage was the direct result of beatings. Other damage was the result of long-term overwork, lack of nutrition, and mental suffering. I developed several chronic illnesses–arthritis, tuberculosis, and high blood pressure. I struggled along the border of life and death for many years. I thought the whole world was very dark and wondered when the light would come. I knew if

I died I would never be able to clear my name for myself, for my children. I knew they could not control my mind.

Qigong saved my life during this difficult time because it comforted my mind and my spirit. I just wanted to keep myself alive so I thought about the need to stay alive for my children and to clear my name. I needed to think positive thoughts and be happy from within myself in spite of the inhumane treatment I was receiving. They could beat me, control me, but they could not control my mind so I did qigong when I was supposed to be sleeping. I was not free, but I had freedom in my mind because qigong let me be calm and let me be in my own world.

I lost eighteen years of what should have been golden times of my life to the Cultural Revolution. Those years are lost forever. Wanting to live for my children helped me to survive the Cultural Revolution and now I have a happy family. I use teaching to make up for the emptiness of those years. In 1999, I established the International Center for Harmony and Living Arts where I currently teach taijiquan, qigong meditation, healthy eating, and about traditional Chinese health culture. I reveal my struggles to American friends so they can understand that taijiquan and qigong are truly tools for healing and for helping anyone moving through the tragedy of grief.

ADVICE TO PASS ON TO OTHERS:

During the Cultural Revolution I faced an unknown future and endured seemingly endless inhumane treatment. I understood the thinking of people who wanted to commit suicide. I asked myself what is the meaning of life? What is the value of keeping alive? I wanted to live. I did not want to die. I knew how important it was for my young son and daughter to have their mother. I wanted to be cleared of the false charges so that future generations would not be burdened with them, I loved life, longed for liberty, and knew I must survive.

Others can take away all of a person's physical freedoms, but they cannot take away the freedoms that exist within one's mind. If you lose your life, that is the worse case. Even if the freedom in your mind is very small it can keep you alive. If you are alive you can dream about loving your family. You can enjoy the blue of the sky and be eager to fly like a bird with wings.

We all need to learn how to take responsibility and try our best. During the time I was sentenced to hard labor on the farm I made friends with two others who were treated as cruelly as me. We attempted to make life bearable for each other. One was a famous artist who was required to do the same hard work I did even though she was pregnant. Her fetus died. She and I developed a simple way to communicate using hand signals–pulling an ear meant one thing, touching a cheek meant another. A sixty-year old man was a professor who had earned a Ph.D in the United States. He was a scholar who could not differentiate between weeds and wheat and when he accidently killed the wheat he was forced to sleep in a pig sty. He knew I wanted to learn English and he put himself at risk by writing English letters in the dirt so I could begin learning.

My advice to anyone who suffers difficulties in sickness, spirit, or life is no matter what hardship and suffering you are experiencing think about what you want to be. What happens is determined by your own will and spirit and not by eternal circumstances. Even on the edge of death you must believe in yourself, cherish your own life, and keep yourself alive. YOU must depend on yourself to protect yourself. Cherish all you have every day, every hour–including the freedom in your inner world. It is also the meaning of your life. You have responsibility for your own life.

There is a Chinese story about the lotus. The lotus has its roots in the mud at the bottom of a lake, but it grows until it reaches the surface of the water. Once in the sunlight the lotus blooms. During the Cultural Revolution my life was mired in mud. I constantly reached for the light in spite of great physical pain and emotional suffering. One day, I reached the sun and my life began to bloom again.

Finding the Positive
Within Illness

Kent

∾

I am in my seventies. I've learned much from my parents
about love, discipline, drive and good work habits. When
I was seventeen, my father died and I felt such loneliness
and anxiety. After a period of confusion, I decided to "pull
up my socks" and get on with life. I've been successful
at several businesses, have enjoyed a happy marriage, and
raised three wonderful daughters. I've also volunteered for
a community foundation for fifteen years. Life has been
good.

In 1994 my world changed when I was diagnosed with
kidney cancer. I went through all the treatments and went
into remission until the year 2000 when I received devastating news. My dormant kidney cancer spread in my
body. I talked with several doctors and they said there was
nothing that they could do for me. They suggested I go to
Boston to a special clinic that worked with kidney patients.
I was given a specific treatment that unfortunately did not
work. However, they offered an experimental program that
I've been in for many weeks. There were fourteen people
in the program and today I am one of three still remaining.

In 2003, the cancer arrested. It seemed like a miracle and I am so delighted, even though my future is unknown and there are no guarantees. These losses, changes and uncertainties have changed my life in regard to values, priorities, mental stamina and appreciation of life.

I have learned I am a man who can be defiant and positive, aggressive and knowledgeable and all in the same breath. All these traits have helped me to live what I consider to be a good life that I will continue to live until it is my time to go.

These are some of the lessons, surprise learnings, and advice:

- You're never too old to learn
- Humility, tolerance, compassion, and respect are a bi-product of my struggle
- Instead of complaining, take control of the situation by learning all you can about the disease and make the final decisions yourself
- Connect with people who talk with you and not at you
- Change your doctor if the chemistry doesn't work and if your questions aren't answered honestly
- Go to the specific hospital and experienced doctor that treats your specific illness
- Ask your doctor what information is available
- Attend support groups
- Understand that men and women may process and deal with their illness differently
- Experience what you are feeling and then take control of your decisions

Loss exists in so many ways and many forms when you have a serious illness. You learn to live with the fact that there are no promises or guarantees in life, In spite of the losses, I can honestly say that there have been positives in facing cancer. My fight with this disease has taught me humility, patience, quietness and keeping a sense of humor. I am grateful for these learnings and have no regrets.

A Howling Ritual
Jeff

∽

My father taught me about howling. He learned to howl from the Indians who lived in the forests of Minnesota where he worked as a lumberjack during the Depression. The howling he taught me was of a special kind. It was only to be used when a dog that was your pet and friend died. My father always had a dog around the house, sometimes two, and occasionally, three. So growing up, I heard a lot of howling.

One of my first memories that I've carried with me all my life was of my father howling. I think I was three or four. My father came into the kitchen in the early evening before dinner and said Duke had died. He was an old dog and had been sick. It was the first time I saw my father sad. He told my mother and me he would be howling that night. I asked to go, but it would be late at night, he said, and I was too little to go. He would tell me about it in the morning.

Late that night I heard him. It was a low wail, soft at first, then slowly it grew louder and louder. I knew it was my father, but it still scared me, but not enough to keep me from sneaking out onto the back porch where he was. He didn't see me at first and continued his howling. I'll never forget the sound. It was pure sadness. I made a noise and he turned. His eyes were full of tears. He smiled and put his arm around me. We sat down and he taught me to howl and told me why.

"It's not just howling, he said. It is a prayer, a prayer of release. You have to howl for three nights, late, so there isn't a lot of everyday noise or anything to interrupt you. You see, a dog is the most loyal creature on earth. When it dies, if it loved its owner, the spirit will remain, too loyal to go to its afterlife. By howling from the heart, you tell your dog's spirit it's okay to go, that it is loved and will always be loved, but it's time to move on. You do this for three nights, and they'll get the message." Then he was quiet, and I knew he was finished. We silently got up, went back in the house and went to bed.

As the years went by, there were more dogs and more howling, but the memory of that first night and the sound of my father's sadness have stayed with me for fifty years.

Long after my father died, I still remembered and kept the tradition he taught me. I had a dog of my own and when he died, I howled for three nights. I let go of my sadness. It was different than with my father. This was my own dog, and I loved it for a long time. It was hard to say good-bye, but the howling felt peaceful and right. Then a strange thing happened. My neighbor's dog heard my howling and started to mourn with me. Then another dog further down the street joined in. Before long, six dogs and myself were howling at the stars and night sky.

After three nights of this chorus, I finished. Bandit heard. He was at peace, and so was I.

ADDENDUM

Grieving Guide

⟨◦⟩

This guide is a reminder of some of the things you can do to ease the pain of grieving. Remember there is always something you can to do soothe yourself. You can add your own thoughts to this list.

- Identify with words what you are experiencing so you don't project your feelings onto others. If you do not communicate honestly, you could manifest angry, curt or apathetic behavior. State your feelings in empowering ways. I need to be alone. I am feeling sad. Would you mind visiting another time? I'm feeling upbeat right now and would prefer not to talk about my loss.
- Tell others directly what you need. I need a hug. Let me cry. Allow me to talk even though I ramble. Can you do an errand?
- Feel your emotions without judgment. If sadness and tears aren't expressed when someone you love dies, when are you supposed to feel sad? You need not apologize to yourself or others for your tears.
- Surround yourself with people who can let you talk, feel, and be who you are during this difficult time. You do not have to express your feelings to

people who are cut off from their own, who exhibit behaviors that tell you they are not interested in listening or who simply advise you to be strong and move on. Remember, the level of comfort people feel with your situation is based on where they have been with their inner journey. Their limitations come from their fear, judgment and unwillingness to experience their vulnerabilities, which they feel could run amok if unloosened.

- Allow yourself the same patience that you've given to others.
- Be honest if someone asks you how you are doing and say, "I'm having some difficult days, as you would expect. Thank you for asking. If I don't call you it's not because I don't care. I need some time alone."
- Set up a tentative schedule for yourself. Devote a certain amount of time to feeling, writing or thinking about your loved one. The rest of the time, plan activities and get-togethers with supportive family or friends. This will help to restore a sense of balance as time moves on.
- Hold off making any major changes or decisions such as a move or a job change. You need to have a chance to adjust to your new circumstances. Discuss it with a professional.
- Rest, rest, rest. You've been on the go. Remember your body and mind need a respite from the whirlwind of emotions you've experienced.
- Contact a lawyer and accountant if you need to settle the deceased's estate or to reassess your financial situation.
- Choose practices that keep feelings flowing and release toxins as you move toward equilibrium.

Among the many disciplines that will help you shift patterns and continue healing are counseling, massage, meditation, physical exercise, music, art, dance, yoga, qigong, prayer, biofeedback, visualization, meditation, acupuncture, traditional and / or complementary medicine, to name a few.

- Acknowledge and appreciate the lessons and new meanings you've received from your experiences.
- Reach out to assist others in their journey once you feel a sense of balance within yourself.

Pass this list on to friends and family.

Resources

❧

American Academy of Bereavement
(*An affiliate of the CMI Education Institute, Inc.*)
P.O. Box 1000
Eau Claire, Wisconsin 54702
1-800-726-3888
Fax: 1-800-554-9775
www.cmieducation.org

American Academy of Medical Acupuncture
1970 East Grand Avenue Suite 330
El Segundo, California 90245
(310) 364-0193
www.medicalacupuncture.org

American Association of Professional Hypnotherapists
16055 SW Walker Road #406
Beaverton, Oregon 97006
(803) 533-7106
www.aaph.org

American Counseling Association
5999 Stevenson Avenue
Alexandria, Virginia 22304

(800) 347-6647
Fax: 1-800- 473-2329
www.counseling.org

American Foundation for Suicide Prevention
120 Wall Street 22nd Floor
New York, New York 10005
(888) 333-AFSP (2377)
Fax: (212) 363-6237
www.afsp.org

American Holistic Medical Association (AHMA)
2366 Commerce Park Suite 101B
Beachwood, Ohio 44122
(216) 292-6644
Fax: (216) 292-6688
www.holisticmedicine.org

American Medical Association
515 North State Street
Chicago, Illinois 60610
(800) 621-8335
www.ama-assn.org

American Psychological Association
750 First Street, N.E.
Washington, D.C. 20002-4242
(800) 374-2721
www.apa.org

American Society for Group Psychotherapy and Psychodrama
301 North Harrison Street Suite 508
Princeton, New Jersey 08540
(609) 737-8500

Fax: (609) 737-8510
www.asgpp.org

American Yoga Association
P.O. Box 19986
Sarasota, Florida 32476
www.americanyogaassociation.org

Association for Death Education and Counseling
111 Deerlake Road Suite 100
Deerfield, Illinois 60015
(847) 509-0403
Fax: (847) 480-9282
www.adec.org

Association for Neuro Linguistic Programming (counseling)
Advanced Communication Training/NLP Center of New York
24 East 12th Street Suite 402
New York, New York 10003
(212) 647-0860
(800) 422-8657
Fax: 1-973-509-2326
www.nlptraining.com

The Center for Loss & Life Transition
3735 Broken Bow Road
Fort Collins, Colorado 80526
(970) 226-6050
Fax: 1-800-922-6051
www.centerforloss.com/pg/default.asp

Center for Mind/Body Studies
5225 Connecticut Avenue NW Suite 414
Washington, D.C. 20015

(202) 966-7338
Fax: (202) 966-2589
www.cmbm.org

Centering Corporation
7230 Maple Street
Omaha, Nebraska 68134
(866) 218-0101
www.centering.org

Grief Digest Magazine and books and resources for
families about loss. Free catalog.
Children's Grief and Loss Issues
www.childrensgrief.net

Children's Grief Education Association
P.O. Box 21876
Denver, Colorado 80221
(303) 722-2319
(877) 722-2319 (toll-free)
www.childgrief.org
"Non-profit organization dedicated to serving the needs of
grieving children and families and to providing education and support to those who serve them"

The Compassionate Friends
P.O. Box 3696
Oak Brook, Illinois 60522-3696
(877) 969-0010
Fax: (630) 990-0246
www.compassionatefriends.org
Newsletter, bibliography, resource guide available

The Cove Center for Grieving Children
250 Pomeroy Ave., Suite 107
Meriden, Ct. 06450
(800) 750-COVE (2683) / (203) 634-0500
www.covect.org
Grief support groups

Degriefing-an approach to grieving (body/mind)
C/O Lyn Prashant M.A., F.T, Ph.D.
P.O. Box 1501
San Anselmo, CA 94979
(415) 457-2272
www.degriefing.com
Workshops

D'Esopo Life Tribute Center /
     D'Esopo Pratt Resource Center
271 Folly Brook Boulevard
Wethersfield, Connecticut 06109
(860) 563-6117 Fax: (860) 563-1943
www.safeplacetogrieve.com

Eye Movement Desensitization Retraining (EMDR)
EMDR-HAP
P.O. Box 6505
Hamden, CT 06517
(203) 288-4450
Fax: (203) 288-4060
www.emdrhap.org
Counseling

EMDR Institute, Inc.
P.O. Box 750
Watsonville, California 95077
(831) 761-1040
Fax: (831) 761-1204
www.emdr.com

Grief & Loss Resource Centre
1045 King Crescent
Golden, BC V0A1H2
ww2.rockies.net/~spirit/grief/grief.html
Hundreds of resources-both on-line and in print-on the
    subjects of grief, loss and bereavement.

GriefNet
P.O. Box 3272
Ann Arbor, Michigan 48106-3272
www.griefnet.org
An Internet community of persons dealing with grief, death and
    major loss

Grief Recovery Online
11877 Douglas Rd.
#102 PMB101
Alpharetta, Georgia 30005
www.groww.com
GROWW offers a wide variety of grief and bereavement
    resources.

Hospice Foundation of America
1-800-854-3402
www.hospicefoundation.org

Institute for Rational Emotive Therapy
45 East 65th Street
New York, New York 10065
(212) 535-0822
Fax: (212) 249-3582
www.rebt.org
Counseling

M.I.S.S.
C/O Joanne Cacciatore, Founder
P.O. Box 5333
Peoria, Arizona 85385-5333
1-888-455-MISS
(623) 979-1000
Fax: (623) 979-1001
www.misschildren.org
Grass roots organization dedicated to the support of parents after
    the death of an infant or child

Mothers Against Drunk Driving
511 East John Carpenter Freeway, #700
Irving, Texas 75062
(800) GETMADD
Fax: (214) 869-2207
www.madd.org

Mt. Ida National Center for Death Education
777 Dedham Street
Newton MA 02459
(617) 928-4649
www.ncde@mountida.edu.

The NAMES Project Foundation
310 Townsend Street Suite 310
San Francisco, California 94107
(415) 882-5500
Fax: (415) 882-6200
www.aidsquilt.org

National Center for Complementary and Alternative
Medicine (NIH)
9000 Rockville Pike
Bethesda, Maryland 20892
www.nccam.nih.gov

National Funeral Directors Association
13625 Bishops Drive
Brookfield, Wisconsin 53005
(800) 228-6332
Fax: (262) 789-6977
www.nfda.org

National Qigong Association
P.O. Box 270065
St. Paul, Minnesota 55127
(888) 815-1893
www.nqa.org

National Thought Field Therapy Association
Susan Connolly Workshops
70 Payne Place Suite #6
Sedona, Arizona 86336
(928) 282-2627
(800) 656-4496
Fax: (928) 282-0121
www.thoughtfieldtherapy.net/tft.pdf

Parents of Murdered Children
100 East 8th Street, B-41
Cincinnati, Ohio 45202
(513) 721-5683
Fax: (513) 345-4489
www.pomc.com

Pen-Parents, Inc.
P.O. Box 8738
Reno, Nevada 89507-8738
Newsletter for bereaved parents/pregnancy/loss/death of a
    child

Sedona Training Associates
60 Tortilla Drive
Sedona, Arizona 86336
(928) 282-3522
1-888-282-5656
Fax: (928) 203-0602
www.sedona.com
Workshops to reduce stress/problem solve

SIDS Alliance
1314 Bedford Avenue Suite 210
Baltimore, Maryland 21208
(800) 221-SIDS
Fax: (410) 653-8709
www.sidsalliance.org
Support for families who have lost an infant to sudden in-
    fant death syndrome

SOS, Survivors of Suicide
www.survivorsofsuicide.com
SOS helps those who have lost a loved one to suicide to
    resolve their grief and pain in their own personal way.

Taylor and Frances Publishers
325 Chestnut Street
Philadelphia, Pennsylvania 19106
(800) 821-8312
www.tandf.co.uk/journals/contact.asp
Death Studies Catalog of current and upcoming books

Widowed Persons Service
C/O AARP
601 East Street, N.W.
Washington, D.C. 20049
(202) 434-2260
www.aarp.org/life/griefandloss
Support programs for widows and widowers. Sponsored
    by AARP

Acknowledgments

❦

A book is never written alone. Everyone I've encountered is my muse. I offer heartfelt thanks to the Atkins, Boggini/ Fisher, Byron, Carnevale, Grundman, Kutzuba, Negrini, Williamee, and Zacconi families. You are the grist for my mill. To those who have given me a spiritual boost: Natlie S, Daling, Lijun and Jean. To my wonderful friends and clients. I thank you for your courage and sharing of your life stories. To all of you who took time to critique this manuscript: Maggie J. (Queen Nudge), Janet, Suzi, Marion, Nancy, Deirdre, Sister Teresa, Shelia, Pat, Jane, Judy and Phyllis. To Nick for his perfect research. To Gwen for her creative suggestions and tireless administrative assistance. To Joy for her generosity of spirit in offering her sage advice and invaluable feedback. It made the difference...and to Sandy Tovray Greenberg for her perpetual guidance, expertise in writing and endless crisp editing...you helped me give birth.

A Special Honoring

David and Susan Williamee Boggini, when in the face of great loss, modeled courage, commitment and responsibility to their children.

18598197R00111

Made in the USA
Middletown, DE
12 March 2015